Donated by

as a service
to
Medical Education

Production Team

Margery H Davis : Peta Dunkley : Ronald M Harden :
Keith Harding : Jennifer M Laidlaw : Arthur M Morris :
Robert A B Wood

Keith Harding, Director of the Wound Healing Research Unit, University of Wales College of Medicine provided much of the content for this programme. In particular the Wound Organiser is his concept, and it forms the basis of the programme. Peta Dunkley, Lecturer in Surgery and Associate Director of the Surgical Skills Unit, University of Dundee, contributed significantly to the content of the programme and wrote the text. General surgical input came from Robert A B Wood, Senior Lecturer in Surgery at the University of Dundee, who has a special interest in wounds and wound healing. Arthur M Morris, Consultant Plastic Surgeon, Dundee Royal Infirmary provided much of the information and photographic material relating to burns and plastic surgery.

Within the Centre for Medical Education, University of Dundee, the programme was produced by Ronald M Harden, Professor of Medical Education and Jennifer Laidlaw, Co-ordinator of Postgraduate Medical and Dental Education. Margery Davis, Lecturer in Medical Education, co-ordinated the project and was responsible for its development.

THE
WOUND
PROGRAMME

Programme Development

A draft version of this programme was read and commented on by

John Collins — Senior Lecturer in Surgery, University of Auckland, New Zealand,

Ian Cree — Senior Lecturer in Pathology, University of Dundee.

Susanta Ghosh — Consultant in Transfusion Medicine, Ninewells Hospital and Medical School.

Members of the ConvaTec Wound Healing Research Institute, Clwyd, Wales.

The draft version was sent to selected medical schools and we are grateful to the following for constructive comments.

Timothy Cooke — St Mungo Professor of Surgery, University of Glasgow

Gerald Davies — Senior Lecturer in Surgery, University of Edinburgh

John G Simpson — and his Curriculum Committee, University of Aberdeen

Photographic Illustrations were provided by

Roger Evans — Consultant in Accident and Emergency Medicine, Cardiff Royal Infirmary.

Keith Harding — Director of the Wound Healing Research Unit, University of Wales College of Medicine.

David Leaper — Senior Lecturer in Surgery, University of Bristol.

Arthur M Morris — Consultant Plastic Surgeon, Dundee Royal Infirmary.

Robert A B Wood — Senior Lecturer in Surgery, University of Dundee.

Medical Illustration Service, University of Dundee.

Some photographic material has been previously published elsewhere and is reproduced by permission.

Jim Glen, Dundee, drew the cartoons.
Maureen Sneddon, Medical Illustration Service, University of Dundee drew the diagrams.

Within the Centre for Medical Education, Dundee, Frances Johnston typed the text, Elsie Jeffrey and Alison Nicoll type-set the programme and Neil Stamper sub-edited it.

Published by the Centre for Medical Education, Dundee in conjunction with Perspective, London. Tel: (44) 382 60111 or (44) 81 788 1766

Printed in Singapore.

Title: The Wound Programme

ISBN 1871 749 239

Copyright © 1992

Contents

Contents of Patient Management Challenges

Contents of "What You Need to Know about Wounds"

The Wound Programme

Start here to find out how to use the programme

Welcome to the Wound Programme

Most health care professionals will be asked at some time for advice on management of a wound. This programme has been designed to help you understand the whole concept of wound healing. Knowledge of how the body responds to an insult and how it repairs resulting damage is fundamental to understanding any disease process. This programme is about injury to skin, but many of the principles can be applied to other tissues.

To understand wound healing, you require knowledge from a wide range of disciplines. It can be difficult to relate what you learn during training to the everyday practice of medicine and this is where this programme can help you. You will be able to appreciate how different disciplines need to be integrated to achieve a successful outcome of clinical problems.

What Will I Gain by Using This Programme?

Benefits of the programme

This programme will enable you to deal with common clinical problems related to wound healing.

You will gain

- the necessary information, including important recent trends.
- an understanding of how this information can be applied to improve patient management.
- the ability to adapt your management to an individual patient's needs, whether in hospital or the community.
- understanding of the role of other health care professionals in the management of wounds.
- an insight into future developments in wound management.

If this type of package is new to you, some questions will need answers.

- *What are the components of the programme?*
- *Where should I start?*
- *How should I keep up to date?*

Let us take each of these questions in turn.

What are the Components of the Programme?

The components

The programme has five components.

Part A   **The reader's guide** - information about the programme and how to use it.

Part B   **Patient management challenges** - an opportunity to manage some patients with wounds and to compare your management decisions with those of experts in the field.

Part C   **"What You Need to Know about Wounds"** - the important facts and ideas you will need to apply when managing patients with wounds.

Part D   **Glossary** - explanation of terminology.

Part E   **Consensus Statement** - a document from the International Committee on Wound Management, an international group of experts, reviewing general principles for the management of patients with wounds.

**Part A
The reader's guide**

You are presently reading the guide, which will enable you to get the best out of the programme.

**Part B
Patient management challenges**

The challenges are designed to highlight essential information, explore important concepts and help you develop appropriate skills and attitudes. Twelve patients are described. They have a variety of problems, some straightforward, others complex. All have a wound as part of their presenting condition. Some problems can be 'solved'. For the more complex problems there is no resolution of the problem and support and advice on coping with the situation are important aspects of management.

How can the patient management challenges help you?

You can use the patient management challenges to

- learn about the topic of wounds
- assess the knowledge you already have
- find out your strengths and weaknesses in the area
- revise the subject.

Design of the Challenges

Information about the patient's problem is presented with an illustration of the wound. A series of questions follows, divided into groups.

 The questions identified by this icon or symbol deal with the structure and function of the skin.

 These questions relate to healing, pathology and microbiology.

 This icon denotes questions about the causes, appearances and management of wounds.

 This icon highlights questions about the special aspects of wounds managed in the community.

 Where you see this icon the questions have been written with experienced practitioners in mind.

You need not have studied the topic to start tackling the patient management challenges. You will be able to work out some of the answers - either from other parts of your training or from experience. If you require guidance to answer the questions you will be referred to the appropriate section in "What You Need to Know about Wounds".

The questions may have more than one answer: you should select the most appropriate for a particular individual. After you have answered a question, turn to the end of the patient management challenge for our specialists' answers. These will direct your attention to important areas. If you do not agree with the specialists' answers or if you do not understand the answer, then look at the pages in "What You Need to Know about Wounds", referenced at the end of the answer. There you will find further information.

Part C "What You Need to Know about Wounds"

The Wound Organiser

This part of the programme provides the information you need when assessing and managing patients with wounds.

The information is presented in the context of a Wound Organiser. It emphasises six aspects which must be considered every time you assess and manage a patient with a wound. These are

- site
- form
- stage
- environment and carer
- cause
- health care systems

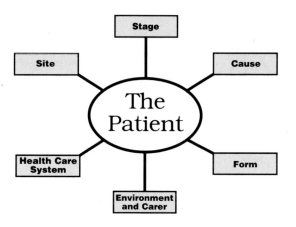

The Wound Organiser

As the Organiser shows, these aspects are all interrelated. Consideration of every aspect will help you devise an individualised solution for your patient.

The Wound Organiser gives you

- a framework for your learning
- a format for the content material
- an Organiser to enable you to assess and manage patients with wounds.

Role of the Organiser

The middle six sections in "What You Need to Know about Wounds" each deal with one aspect of the Organiser. A short introductory section explains the significance of the topic. A final section deals with the toolkit currently available to practitioners to manage wounds. Some sections start with a summary chart giving an overview of its contents.

Each page is self-contained and deals with one important concept stated in the page heading.

This short sentence explains how the page relates to preceding and succeeding pages.

Some pages contain an illuminating comment.

The Wound Organiser

xxxxxxxxx
xxxxxxxxxx

Most pages contain a visual illustration of the concept - a photograph, diagram or cartoon.

X x x x x x x x x
x x x x x x x x x

Icons flag up text in different categories.

Structure and function of skin.

Clinical aspects of wounds.

Healing, pathology and microbiology of wounds.

Advanced information - for the more experienced practitioner or the reader wishing to make a special study of the topic.

Wound management in the community.

Any references to further information sources at the bottom of the page are marked by a key word from the main text, followed by the open book symbol.

Questions to make you think, and apply some of the newly gained information to existing knowledge and experience.

G

xx
xx

This column is used to cross-reference information within "What You Need to Know about Wounds". There are three types of cross-referencing.

Individual words may be cross-referenced to the glossary, at the end of the programme. The word is followed by the glossary symbol.

Cross-references to key words and page numbers show where related material occurs in "What You Need to Know About Wounds".

The open book symbol marks topics on which further information is given at the foot of the page.

**Part D
Glossary**

One of the most difficult aspects of starting any new topic is grasping the terminology. The glossary lists, in alphabetical order, terms that may be unfamiliar, with a concise definition. The numbers which follow are the pages on which that term is used. Wherever such a term appears in the text of "What You Need to Know about Wounds", it is repeated in the right-hand margin followed by 'G'.

**Part E
Consensus
Statement**

This document sets out guidelines for the management of patients with wounds and provides an overview of the current situation. It was formulated by the International Committee on Wound Management, an interdisciplinary, multi-professional group with expertise throughout the field of wound management. Page numbers of relevant paragraphs in "What You Need to Know about Wounds" are cross-referenced in the margin.

Where Should I Start?

Using the package

This learning material is not a textbook, but a flexible learning resource adaptable to user needs.

- Start with the patient management challenges. We recommend this, for enjoyment and stimulation. Tackle the challenges alone or, even better, as a group - exchange ideas and information with others. The challenges are designed to cover the most important aspects of the topic. Completing the challenges should give you systematic coverage of the topic of wounds and wound healing.

- If you wish to concentrate on one aspect of the topic, select the questions identified by the icon for the aspect listed on page 9. The diagram below will help you select the option most appropriate to your needs.

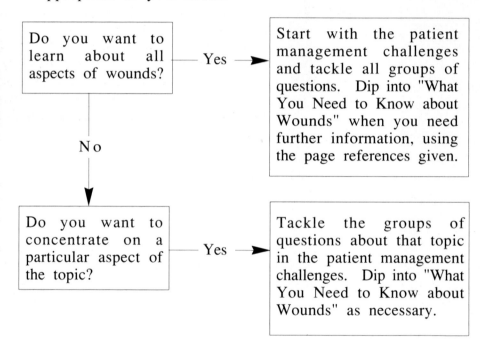

Do you want to learn about all aspects of wounds? — Yes → Start with the patient management challenges and tackle all groups of questions. Dip into "What You Need to Know about Wounds" when you need further information, using the page references given.

No ↓

Do you want to concentrate on a particular aspect of the topic? — Yes → Tackle the groups of questions about that topic in the patient management challenges. Dip into "What You Need to Know about Wounds" as necessary.

- Alternatively, you could read the information in "What You Need to Know about Wounds", then assess your grasp of it by tackling the patient management challenges. Remember this is not designed to read sequentially and may take some time, particularly for those new to the subject. This approach may be most useful for experienced health care professionals wishing to revise the subject, who can read through the material quickly. Or you could start by reading a section in "What You Need to Know about Wounds", appropriate to the discipline you are studying at present. Then, browse through other sections, following the appropriate icon, or cross-references.

- Select the appropriate starting section from the contents list. We have included summary charts at the start of many sections. Use these for an overview of the contents of the section. Then go on to assess your grasp of the information by tackling the appropriate questions in the patient management challenges. Remember these are identified by the icon illustrating the subject to which they refer.

This diagram will help you select the option most appropriate to your needs.

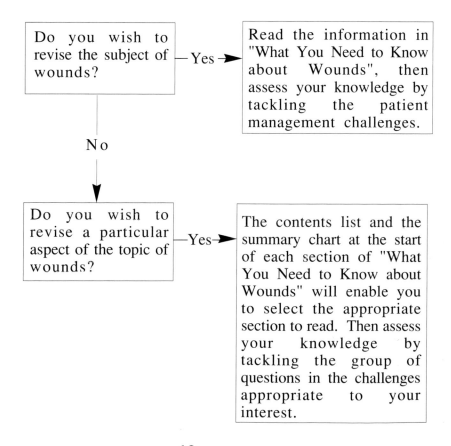

Do you wish to revise the subject of wounds?	—Yes→	Read the information in "What You Need to Know about Wounds", then assess your knowledge by tackling the patient management challenges.

No

Do you wish to revise a particular aspect of the topic of wounds?	—Yes→	The contents list and the summary chart at the start of each section of "What You Need to Know about Wounds" will enable you to select the appropriate section to read. Then assess your knowledge by tackling the group of questions in the challenges appropriate to your interest.

How Should I Keep Up to Date?

Learning is ongoing

Once you have completed this programme, we hope that you will want to keep up-dating your knowledge of wounds and wound healing. You can do this in several ways.

- **Working with experienced health care professionals**

  You may, in other parts of your training, see experienced professionals treat wounds. Take the opportunity to discuss wounds with them. If possible, assess and manage wounds yourself, for instance by helping in casualty or working in the wards. You will gain much from this level of practical involvement.

- **Projects**

  Some of you will have projects and dissertations to complete. Using this programme as a starting point, choose the topic of wounds as an area for further research. This could be in a hospital or community setting. After working through this programme you may wish to study a particular aspect in more detail. Approach a health care professional, experienced in the management of wounds, for advice.

- **Further reading**

  Many journals deal specifically with the topic of wound management e.g. The Journal of Wound Care and Wounds.

  You may find these books useful reference resources.

  Wound Healing for Surgeons. Bucknall T E and Ellis H (eds). London, Bailiere Tindall, 1984.

  Wound Healing: Biochemical and Clinical Aspects. Cohen I K, Diegelmann R F and Luidblod W. W B Saunders, 1991. (ISBN/ISSN 0721625749)

  Wound Healing. Janssen H, Rooman R and Robertson J I S (eds.). Janssen Biomedical Science Series. Petersfield Wrightson Biomedical, 1991.

The Wound Programme

Compare your management decisions with those of experts

15

Patient's History

Janet Dawson

Leg ulcer present for two years

Janet Dawson is a 77 year old widow. She is 5' 3" tall and weights 85 kg. She lives on her own on the ninth floor of a multistorey block of flats. Her only medical problem relates to long-standing bilateral varicose veins and associated varicose eczema. She is not on any medication. Her only child, a mentally retarded son, with whom she lived, died suddenly some years ago. Since then she has had few visitors.

During a routine check-up, she drew her doctor's attention to a lesion just above the medial maleolus of her left leg. She first noticed it after she tripped over a rug at home and fell. At the time it seemed trivial, requiring only a sticking plaster, but it failed to heal. Her doctor sent her to the practice nurse to deal with the wound, where it was dressed with paraffin gauze, dry gauze and tape. When the nurse saw the patient again, the leg was noted to be oedematous. The wound seemed slightly larger and the nurse described it as a leg ulcer. She arranged to see the patient again and tried a variety of topical treatments over the next two years without success. The nurse is a pleasant talkative person who had been involved in treating the patient's son in the past. She often chatted with Mrs Dawson after dressing her leg.

When the nurse is on holiday, you, a newly qualified general practitioner, are asked to look at the patient's leg and advise on how to proceed with her care. The appearance of the leg is shown in the photograph.

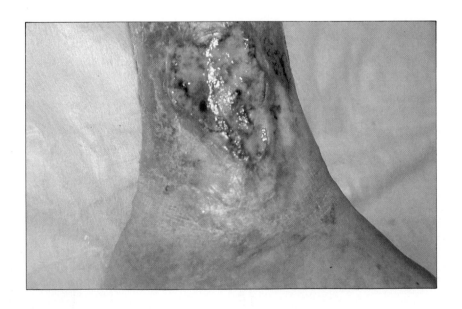

Janet Dawson

Solve the problems with the help of your resource book

1	Which facets of the Organiser are of particular importance in assessing the reasons for non-healing of this lesion?	10, 77, 87, 93, 121, 122, 123, 131, 139, 141, 155
2	What investigations should be carried out on this patient?	104, 105, 106, 121, 124
3	How would you proceed to manage her leg ulcer?	122, 123, 131, 154, 171
4	What reasons can you suggest for a lesion in this position failing to heal?	122, 123
1	What do you think will be the effects of the barrier function of the skin being breached?	81
1	Since bacteria colonise the skin and its wounds how would you decide if this lesion was infected in a clinically significant way?	94, 104, 105
2	How would you identify organisms present in this wound?	98, 104
1	What effect do you think regular visits from the nurse may have had on Mrs Dawson's life?	131
2	What advice does the patient need regarding community/social facilities that may be available to her?	131, 145, 150

Specialists' views on pages 18 - 20

Specialists' Views

Janet Dawson

Related information can be found in Part C

1 Healing of wounds is a complex issue and many factors need to be taken into account. This programme describes an Organiser in which six key issues are identified. All need to be considered. The **site** of the wound is of importance as the skin in this area is prone to injury. The blood supply to skin of the lower leg may be poor in the elderly. In this patient varicose veins will have resulted in venous hypertension. The wound is at the proliferative **stage** of healing, which has been prolonged as a result of venous hypertension, and possibly, by ineffective treatment. Although the initial **cause** of the wound was trauma, it failed to heal and became a chronic wound. In **form** it is a large flat wound, not obviously infected at present. However, it is likely that episodes of infection may have been responsible for its increase in size from the original minor injury to its current appearance.

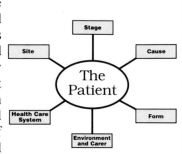

The Wound Organiser

Mrs Dawson's **environment** has profound implications for the outcome of treatment. In particular her social isolation makes rest and elevation of the leg difficult. The apparent beneficial effects of the nurse's visits to relieve her social isolation may have adversely affected her motivation to achieve healing. About 1% of patients with chronic leg ulcers are known to use the wound as a passport to achieve social contact. The priorities set by the **health care system** determine the distribution of resources. Had the health care system had unlimited resources it may have allowed for the intensive management of this patient, with a speedier resolution of the problem. This is not practicable in most health care systems.

2 Several investigations are indicated.

FBC	To look for anaemia and a raised WBC .
ESR	Used to screen for an inflammatory process as a cause of ulceration
Random blood sugar estimation	To screen for diabetes mellitus.

10, 77, 87, 93, 121, 122, 123, 131, 139, 141, 155

104, 105, 106, 121, 124

Tests of renal function and of liver function, to include serum proteins particularly albumin, may be indicated in patients with oedematous legs or if there is relevant previous medical history. If a Doppler flow meter is available, a Doppler ankle/brachial pressure index should be performed. A pressure index of less than 0.8 indicates problems with arterial supply to the lower limb. A pressure index of greater than 0.8 indicates that any healing problems are probably not due to arterial supply. Mrs Dawson's pressure index is 0.95, indicating the ulcer is probably venous in origin. If you are concerned about a subclinical infection a wound swab should be taken, but it is important to correlate the bacteriology results with the clinical features. The wound may be colonised by many organisms with different sensitivities but the patient does not require oral antibiotics if there is no sign of spreading infection, such as cellulitis.

3 Successful treatment requires adequate compression bandaging of the leg, from the toes to mid/upper thigh. Later compression stockings must be accurately fitted to give even pressure. Factors influencing this treatment are

122, 123, 131, 164, 171

   a) availability of bandages and stockings in the community.
   b) acceptability of such compression to the patient and nurse.
   c) the need for a nurse to reapply the compression bandaging.
   d) frequency of nursing visits.

A wound contact material such as a hydrocolloid, or alginate, is necessary to protect the wound from trauma, bacterial invasion, desiccation, to control exudate and pain and to promote healing. This patient is obese and requires a calorie controlled diet to reduce her weight. She should also be given dietary advice to maintain adequate nutrition. In some specialist centres compression devices may be available. She should maintain social mixing. Mrs Dawson should be visited regularly by the general practitioner. If following these measures, the ulcer fails to heal, or increases in size, then ideally a period of bed rest in hospital will be required.

4 Varicose ulcers are difficult to heal because of localised oedema caused by venous hypertension. This may lead to deposition of fibrin around capillaries. White cell function in an ulcerated limb has been shown to be disordered. Factors predisposing to venous hypertension include varicose veins due to damaged valves, e.g. DVT, or inherited absence or abnormality of these valves. This leads to inefficiency of the muscular pump system of venous return causing reflux of blood from deep to superficial veins at high pressure. This abnormality is even more marked in the upright posture, particularly at rest.

122, 123

1 Entry of bacteria is permitted which may lead to infection. There will also be fluid loss - the wound will 'weep'. There may be occasional bleeding.

81

1 You would look for the local signs of intense inflammation - heat, redness, pain, swelling, loss of function, and/or for pus. She might also have systemic effects if this infection reaches the bloodstream.

94, 104, 105

2 Identification of organisms present in this wound is achieved by taking a bacteriological swab from the wound and growing any organism(s) present. Subcultures will isolate the organism. Gram stain and other tests will help identify the organism. You are likely to grow a number of organisms, some of which may not be clinically significant. Clinically this wound is not infected. The pink skin around the wound is newly formed epithelium and not cellulitis. The slightly adherent slough consists of mainly dead white cells and does not constitute an excessive, infected discharge.

98, 104

1 Regular contact with the nurse relieved the social isolation of the patient's life. Patients such as Mrs Dawson may become dependent on their wounds for social contact. On occasion, they may even prevent healing to prolong this contact.

131

2 With this patient, personal and family factors, professional and voluntary agencies all can contribute to reducing her social isolation. The patient's personality and her attitude to mixing with others are very important. The advantages of social contact with others should be pointed out to her. If she is still unwilling to mix with strangers she may be able to obtain support from family members. Siblings, cousins, etc may be willing to visit and acceptable to the patient.

131, 145, 150

Various professional organisations may provide support in this case. The general practitioner may be able to provide a specialist health visitor for the elderly. The numbers of such visitors are increasing in the community in the UK. Social workers may be able to offer some help, and she may be eligible for Meals On Wheels or a home carer. Referral to a consultant geriatrician may lead to facilities at a day hospital being made available. She may also be eligible for a range of other social and medical benefits to aid independent living. In occasional cases admission to hospital may be appropriate. Voluntary organisations such as charities, church groups and neighbourhood groups may also be able to offer assistance to this patient.

Patient's History

Frederick Brown is an 82 year old retired banker. He is 6' 2" tall, weighs 63 kg and is of lean build. He lives with his 80 year old wife who is now rather frail and is dependent on him for dressing and daily living. He remained well and played an occasional game of golf until he developed a severe left-sided hemiparesis necessitating hospital admission.

On admission he had profound weakness of his left arm and leg and was incontinent of urine. The urinary incontinence continued and 48 hours after admission he was catheterised. He developed a bronchopneumonia which was treated with appropriate antibiotic therapy and physiotherapy. For a period of two days he was critically ill and nursed in a high dependency unit. On return to the ward four days after admission, redness over the sacrum was noted but no action was taken. By two weeks after admission he had the wounds shown in the photograph. The levels of exudate and odour from the larger wound were considerable.

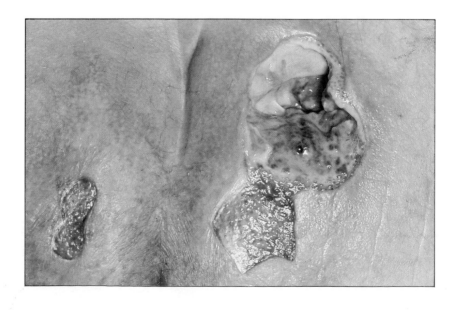

Patient Management Challenge - 2

Frederick Brown

Solve the problems with the help of your resource book

	1	How, on admission, would you assess the risk of this patient developing a pressure sore?	127, 132
	2	What steps should have been taken on admission to prevent a pressure sore developing?	127
	3	What steps should you take to promote healing of this sore?	126, 127, 138, 139
	1	What structures do you think are involved in the lesions shown in the photograph?	82
	2	When lying flat on his back in bed, what areas does Mr Brown subject to increased pressure?	125
	3	What factors may have contributed towards the development of this lesion?	81, 125, 132
	1	What laboratory investigations might be appropriate when considering this patient's wound?	104, 105, 106, 121,
	2	How does the body remove dead tissue from a wound?	96
	3	By what method will these sores heal?	83, 85, 93, 126
	4	If the pressure sore is not healing as expected three months later, what local complications in the wound should be excluded?	129
	1	What assistance might be available to Mr and Mrs Brown on his return home?	150
	2	How might the community nurse help in this case?	149

Specialists' views on pages 24 - 25

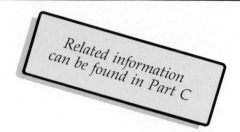

1 Mr Brown is in a high risk category for developing pressure sores because of his age, build, immobility and incontinence. The risk could be fully assessed using a scoring system such as Norton's or Waterlow's.   **127, 132**

2 Steps to control his incontinence should have been taken on admission.   These include the use of urodome or catheterisation.   Frequent turning and inspection of high risk areas should have been instituted.   Management should include using specialised beds which are available for relieving and redistributing pressure.   High staff to patient ratios, for turning patients, rank above specialised apparatus in importance and may be found in high dependency areas. However, it is not always practical to turn patients, e.g. one with a pelvic fracture, without specialised apparatus.   **127**

3 Both local and general measures are required to promote healing.   **127, 138, 139**

Local Measures

The first step is to cleanse the wound, debride dead tissues and control any infection.   Irrigation of the cavity with fluid such as saline will remove loose material, pus and exudate. The cavity can then be filled with a dressing material such as a hydrogel or hydrocolloid paste to promote autolytic debridement.   If dead tissues are clearly visible, surgical debridement is appropriate.   Cleaning the wound will aid speedier healing.   When this has been achieved, a decision should be made either to allow the wound to heal by granulation and epithelialisation by continuing the moist healing regime or, if the wound is large and deep enough, to consider plastic surgery.   Special knowledge and ability to raise skin flaps may be required.

General Measures

The priority is to relieve pressure on the area of the pressure sore and other weight bearing areas.   Measures to achieve this include good nursing practice such as regular turning, dealing with the disability caused by his stroke, ensuring adequate nutrition, intensive physiotherapy to promote mobilisation and rehabilitation, and continued use of appropriate pressure relieving surfaces while still immobile.

1 Skin, subcutaneous tissue and gluteal muscle are involved in these lesions.   **82**

2 The scalp, scapulae, thoracic spinous processes, elbows, sacrum and heels are all subject to increased pressure.   **125**

3 The potential for damaging pressure effects on the skin is increased by the patient's immobility. Skin breakdown is more likely because of maceration of the skin if the patient is incontinent of either urine or faeces. Concomitant infection, an episode of hypotension, malnutrition and profound debility also increase the potential for pressure sore development.

81, 125, 132

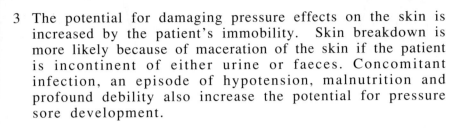

1 On admission, Hb, WBC, ESR, measurement of renal and liver function, including serum proteins particularly albumin should have been performed. If his diet had been poor prior to admission, he may have a low haemoglobin and albumin, both of which would have a detrimental effect on wound healing. A base line white blood count and ESR would be useful parameters for monitoring wound infection, although the development of bronchopneumonia would influence these results. Interpretation of a raised ESR in the elderly may be difficult, but when there is a move from a normal to raised level, a cause must be sought.

104, 105, 106, 121

A wound swab should be performed and repeated as necessary. A radiograph of the sacrum should be taken to look for osteomyelitis if there is persistent infection in a long-standing pressure sore.

2 The body removes dead tissue by the process of autolysis. Naturally occurring enzymes digest debris producing a plane of separation between viable and non-viable tissue.

96

3 If there is no surgical intervention, secondary healing will take place, leaving a scar.

83, 85, 93, 126

4 In this patient, osteomyelitis and the much rarer secondary amyloidosis should be excluded.

129

1 If no family member is available to look after them at home, they are unlikely to be able to manage alone and may have to enter a residential or nursing home. If a family member is available, allowances may be claimed by the patient in view of the probable severity of disability. Depending on degree of recovery from hemiparesis, Mr Brown may require special aids, e.g. mattress or a seat. If any adaptations to the home are needed, he may be eligible (depending on means) for a grant paid by social services. Day centres may be provided in some areas by social services. Independent agencies, e.g. Crossroads, supply non-qualified carers who will sit with the disabled. Respite admissions of up to two weeks in hospital are available to allow carers to go on holiday.

150

2 In the UK the community nurse will be able to dress the patient's wound, encourage re-mobilisation, monitor family ability to cope and liaise with other agencies.

149

Kathy Melville

The infected diabetic foot

Kathy Melville is a 47 year old hospital pharmacist. She is an insulin dependent diabetic who has been meticulous with her diabetic control since diagnosis 20 years ago. She has regularly attended the diabetic clinic. However, she has developed a peripheral neuropathy. Kathy sustained unrecognised trauma to the sole of her right foot (possibly from wearing ill-fitting new shoes, or from walking without footwear at home). When she realised there was a lesion present, although it seemed trivial, she sought advice from her general practitioner who prescribed oral antibiotics. Kathy assiduously carried out adequate cleansing and dressing. She also avoided further trauma to the foot. However, over the weeks, the lesion failed to heal and in fact became larger and deeper.

She returned five weeks later to her general practitioner. The worsening situation caused him to refer her immediately to the diabetic clinic. Investigations performed included an FBC. The WCC was 17,000, predominantly neutrophils. The ESR was 75. A plain X-ray of the right foot showed changes consistent with osteomyelitis of the fourth and fifth right metatarsals. Kathy was admitted to hospital for excision of these metatarsals.

Post-operatively she did well initially. However, on the seventh post-operative day she developed a pyrexia and her diabetic control deteriorated. When you, the surgical house officer, were called to see her you noted swelling above the bandaging on her right foot. When the dressings were removed, the wound was surrounded by cellulitis and the tissues engorged as shown in the photograph.

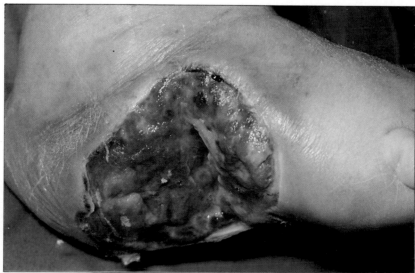

Cavity wound, with surrounding cellulitis and engorged tissues, on side of right foot. Fourth and fifth metatarsals have been removed.

Patient Management Challenge - 3

Solve the problems with the help of your resource book

1	Why did the problem in her foot not bring Kathy to see the general practitioner sooner?	86
2	Why is Kathy more likely to develop infection than non-diabetic patients in a similar situation?	86, 128
3	Why were the metatarsals removed? What general principles of wound management had been applied.	105, 141, 161
4	How would you monitor progress towards healing in Kathy's wound?	
1	What physiological mechanisms do we normally use to prevent damage to the skin?	86
1	Describe the pathological sequence of events, from the original injury to the development of osteomyelitis.	128
2	What bacteriological investigations would be appropriate at the stage shown in the photograph?	104
3	Which bacteria might be isolated from the wound in the photograph and which are likely to be clinically significant?	104
4	What pathological response is responsible for the swollen, red appearance of the wound?	94
1	What advice would you give to diabetics to avoid this sequence of events?	128, 159
2	How much of a problem are foot complications in diabetes?	128, 159
3	What professional help might the patient require on her return home?	148, 149, 150
4	If Kathy had been self-employed, what problems would she have faced with rehabilitation?	145

Specialists' views on pages 28 - 29

Specialists' Views

Kathy Melville

Related information can be found in Part C

1 Because of her diabetic peripheral neuropathy, Kathy did not experience pain in her foot and was unaware of the developing problem. Peripheral neuropathy is more common in poorly controlled diabetics but still occurs in about 20% of well controlled diabetics. | **86**

2 Her diabetes makes her more prone to infection. The peripheral neuropathy means she is more likely to be clumsy and to sustain unperceived trauma. This allows ingress of infection and its development to a serious stage before she becomes aware of it. She may also have developed microvascular complications of diabetes, further compromising tissue viability. | **86, 128**

3 It is difficult to eradicate infection from bone, because of its poor cortical blood flow. An established osteomyelitis often leads to bone death. Combined infection and the presence of dead bone (sequestrum) delay healing. That is why surgical debridement of this wound was carried out by removing the metatarsals and other necrotic tissues. Removal of infected and necrotic tissue creates a wound with free drainage and allows healing by secondary intention. | **141, 161**

4 You should measure the wound dimensions frequently, to establish that the wound is becoming smaller. You should also watch Kathy walking, as special shoes may be needed for her to return to normal walking. She may need some time to adapt to these shoes. It is important to maintain good diabetic control and to prevent further wound infection developing. Taking a history, measuring the temperature and carrying out plain X-rays of the foot, ESR, WBC, and white cell scan, if available, may all be employed to monitor for recurrence of osteomyelitis. | **128**

1 Pressure sensors in the skin normally give warning and prevent damage. Pain fibres also give warnings and initiate a withdrawal reflex. Normally we are unconsciously and continuously moving under such stimuli, even when asleep. | **86**

1 The sequence of events probably started with minor trauma from walking without footwear. This produced tissue damage and breached the skin's protective barrier, allowing ingress of infection. The resulting infection (to which diabetics are more prone) was unnoticed, due to lack of sensation. The infection then progressed to involve deeper structures, including bone. | **128**

2 A wound swab should be taken for aerobic and anaerobic culture, and antibiotic sensitivities. It is likely that a number of organisms will be identified, but some will be of greater clinical significance than others (see answer to next question). Blood cultures should also be performed, to look for evidence of systemic infection. It is important to let the bacteriology laboratory know what antibiotics the patient has been given. Where feasible, tissue biopsy and culture would be the most accurate method of establishing the infecting organism. **104**

3 Skin commensals are likely to colonise wounds. Staphylococci, streptococci, anaerobes and gram negative organisms may also be isolated. **104**

Staphylococcus aureus, group A streptococci, or anaerobes are the most likely cause of this infection, with group A streptococci more usually associated with cellulitis.

4 This wound is surrounded by cellulitis, the clinical description for an intense diffuse inflammatory response to infection of the skin and soft tissues. The inflammatory process consists of vasodilation, increased capillary permeability and vasoactive mediator release caused by locally released vasoactive factors. Some of these increase temperature, cause redness, swelling, pain, loss of function and give systemic effects. **94**

1 Diabetics should be advised to avoid pressure or trauma to their feet and to wear only well fitting shoes. Good diet and diabetic control, good care of the feet with access to chiropody services and regular inspection of the feet are all important. Immediate medical attention should be sought if any suspicion of abnormality develops. **128, 159**

2 Diabetic foot complications are the commonest cause for admission of diabetics to hospital. **128, 159**

3 Medical help might be needed to deal with further episodes of infection and to maintain diabetic control. Nursing help might be necessary for managing wound dressings and protecting the wound. Ancillary help may be required if special appliances, eg altered shoes or crutches, are needed. **148, 149, 150**

4 As she is a UK hospital pharmacist, she will be able to take time off work - up to six months on full pay. If she had been self-employed, she would have suffered loss of income unless she had private insurance. Financial pressure might have induced her to return to work sooner than is desirable. This should be recognised as an important factor in compliance for some patients. **145**

Patient's History

Raj Patel

A wound where contamination is unavoidable

Raj Patel is a healthy 27 year old restaurant owner. He is known to have had a pilonidal sinus in the natal cleft for some time, following the development of an abscess which settled on oral antibiotic therapy. He has no other previous medical history of note, and lives with his wife and two young children in good social circumstances. He went to see his general practitioner with pain at the bottom of his spine. There was nothing to see on examination but he was given oral amoxycillin in view of his past history. However, two days later he was in severe pain and returned to his general practitioner. This time, on examination there was a fluctuant swelling in the natal cleft. As the infection had not settled on oral antibiotic therapy, emergency admission to hospital was arranged. On the evening of admission he was taken to theatre. The abscess was excised and all apparent sinus tracts were removed. The wound was packed. Raj Patel appeared very anxious on the day after his operation. He was sent home 48 hours after surgery.

Three weeks later you, as the new surgical house officer are contacted by his general practitioner. She is concerned by the appearance of the wound. You agree to see him on the ward and you find the wound has the appearance shown in the photograph.

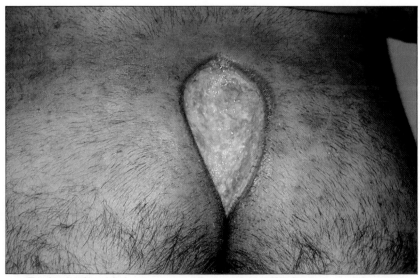

Excised pilonidal abscess with a yellow (fibrinous) membrane.

Raj Patel

Solve the problems with the help of your resource book

1   Does the yellow appearance in the base of the wound signify infection?

98

2   How would you use the Wound Organiser, in caring for Raj Patel?

10, 77, 120, 138, 160, 166

3   What problems related to his wound would Raj Patel have had in the post-operative period? Suggest how you could help him with these problems.

138, 170

4   Raj Patel appeared very anxious when seen on the day after his operation on the ward round. What do you think are the possible causes of this anxiety related to his wound? How would you explore them with him?

137, 146, 170

5   What is the most appropriate dressing to use for this wound, bearing in mind patient acceptability?

138, 163, 169

1   Why do you think antibiotic therapy was unsuccessful in preventing this abscess?

120, 172

2   What processes will this wound go through when healing?

98

Specialists' views on pages 32 - 33

Raj Patel

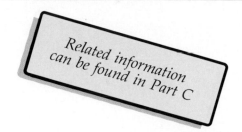

Related information can be found in Part C

98

The wound looks as if it is healing well. The appearance of a yellow surface to a wound is not necessarily an adverse development. In this case, it is fibrinous membrane, seen in many healthy normally healing acute wounds and it is not a cause for concern. It should be noted that there is no evidence of cellulitis.

10, 77, 120, 138, 160, 166

The Wound Organiser can be used to assess and manage patients such as Raj Patel. The **site** gives rise to special sources of anxiety, discussed later. The wound and dressings are liable to contamination from the bowel. This influences dressing selection and frequency of replacement. This is a three week post-operative acute wound, in the proliferative **stage of healing** by granulation. The **cause** of the wound is surgical. As there was

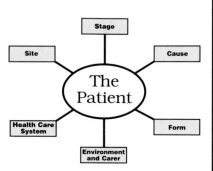

The Wound Organiser

pre-existing infection, in the initial stages, there will be a marked inflammatory exudate. Dressings, therefore, should promote granulation and should also be absorbent. The clinical **form** is a cavity wound and the dressing chosen should maintain good drainage. Apart from the initial post-operative period in hospital, Raj Patel may have to manage the wound by **himself** in the home **environment**. He will need to wash the area and change dressings frequently. In his social circumstances, this does not present a problem. However, for some people, ready and frequent access to a bath or shower is not possible.

138, 170

He is likely to have had pain, particularly when changing the dressing or sitting. Analgesics for pain relief are indicated. Pain from the wound can also be reduced by using an appropriate dressing. Adherent dressings which cause pain when removed are to be avoided. A suitable dressing might be silicone foam. It is important to position Mr Patel with cushions so that when seated, he is not putting direct pressure on the wound. To reduce pain when his bowels open, use a faecal softening agent and a high roughage diet. These measures will also counteract the constipating effect of the analgesics. He might complain of discharge from the wound particularly in the first two weeks, and itch caused by allergy to tape or by intraepidermal candida infection. Faecal contamination of a wound in this position is also a problem. Washing the wound after defecation is advised.

4 The sources of anxiety are likely to be worry about the pain, particularly when his bowels open, and worry about the possible effects on the wound of straining at stool. He may also be concerned about bedding and clothes being soiled with wound discharge. Not being able to return to work may be a concern, as he is self-employed. He will want to know how long the wound will take to heal and whether it may recur.

He needs reassurance about adequate pain relief and explicit instructions about keeping his stools soft and achieving a regular bowel motion. Anxiety about bowel coming out of the wound, if expressed, can also be dealt with by reassurance. If he works with food in his restaurant, he cannot return to work until the wound is healed. A wound this size is likely to take six to eight weeks to heal. If his work does not involve food handling, he might be able to return to work before complete healing takes place. He should also know that further surgery may be necessary. The risk of recurrence in this disease is considerable and figures of 15% at five years have been quoted.

137, 146, 170

5 Traditionally, gauze has been used to dress wounds such as these. It tends to adhere if not changed frequently. The patient may find daily changing and packing both painful and inconvenient. Modern wound management materials, such as silicone foam or alginate dressings, may avoid this. However, they may well need to be applied by the district or practice nurse. He should be seen weekly in the outpatient department to check that healing is progressing as expected.

138, 163, 169

1 An abscess is a collection of pus. As the blood supply to its centre is poor, antibiotic penetration is limited. The causative organism may not have been sensitive to the antibiotic. The antibiotic may also have been given too late in the inflammatory process.

120, 172

2 The wound will heal by granulation tissue formation, wound contraction and epithelialisation.

98

Patient's History

Florence Tindall is a frail 82 year old, who lives on her own. She has congestive cardiac failure, poorly controlled by bendrofluazide 10 mg daily. She also has mild renal impairment.

Miss Tindall has good neighbours who visit her every day and bring her occasional meals. She manages to do her own shopping but recently while returning home heavily laden with shopping, she injured her right leg. She tripped over a kerb and gashed her leg on an uneven paving slab.

She was taken home by a passer-by and attempted to manage the wound herself. However, four hours later, as the wound was bleeding and becoming more painful she went to the accident and emergency department of her local hospital where you the casualty officer are called to see her. The wound on her leg is shown in the photograph.

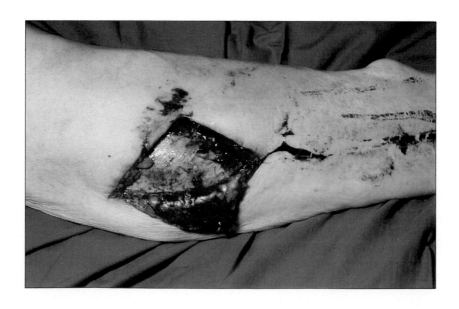

Patient Management Challenge - 5

Florence Tindall

Solve the problems with the help of your resource book

1	What are the options to effect closure of the wound?	**162**
2	In this case, what are the problems associated, with the various methods of closure?	**113, 162**
3	What complications may arise from a pre-tibial laceration?	**113, 122, 123**
1	What anatomical and physiological features are likely to slow the rate of healing in this case?	**107, 103**
2	Is the skin over your shin thicker or thinner than the skin of your: a) eyelid? b) back?	
	Florence Tindall sustained a serious wound from minor trauma to her skin. Would you expect a young person to sustain a similar wound from such trauma?	**84**
1	What is a haematoma? What makes haematoma formation more likely in this patient?	**91, 140**
2	Would the presence of haematoma predispose to any other complication?	**91, 103, 105**
3	If you were able to examine this patient's wound microscopically three weeks after the injury, what would you see?	**93, 98, 99, 107**
1	What are the implications of such an injury for the patient's lifestyle?	**144, 145**
2	In the UK what advantages and disadvantages are there for her treatment being supervised: a) by the accident and emergency department? b) by the community nurse?	**147, 148**

Specialists' views on pages 36 - 37

Related information can be found in Part C

1 As the area of undermined skin is small and the skin edge appears viable the options are primary closure by

- suturing
- suture strips

If the flap appears non-viable, skin graft as a primary procedure may be carried out.

162

2   i) The wound could be closed primarily with sutures, but these are likely to tear the skin because of the patient's age and the site. A combination of sutures and suture strips is possible.

   ii) Suture strips alone may be used to retain the skin in position once the wound has been cleansed. A non-adherent dressing should be used covered by a firm support dressing, left undisturbed for one week.

Suture strips are probably the best option, because they help to narrow the gap to be healed, although there is still a danger of them tearing the skin. Marginal necrosis of the primarily closed wound can occur. This can then be allowed to heal by secondary intention with dressings. If no progress towards healing is seen in the next four weeks, a skin graft should be considered. If it is not possible to approximate the wound edges because of excessive tension, the remaining skin deficit can be covered with a skin graft. If the gap is narrow it can be allowed to heal by secondary intention.

Skin grafting may require admission to hospital. The grafted skin does not always take fully and potential problems can develop at the donor site.

113, 162

3 The likely complications are haematoma formation, infection, and oedema. A compression dressing with rest and elevation of the leg will help to prevent haematoma and oedema formation. A support bandage e.g. elasticated tubular bandage from toe to knee would be important to help prevent further injury and oedema. It should be applied for several weeks.

113, 122, 123

1 Healing in a limb may be impaired by local factors such as infection, alterations to blood flow and oedema. In addition, general factors such as the age of the patient, tissue age and reduced sensation must also be considered.

103, 107

2 The thickness of the skin over your shin is likely to be intermediate between that of your eyelid and that of your back. This relates to the dermal thickness.

84

A young person is unlikely to sustain such severe injury from such minor trauma as younger skin is thicker, stronger and more elastic. The development of a bruise or minor abrasion is more likely.

1   Haematoma is a collection of blood or blood clot in the tissues. Blood vessels in the elderly are more brittle than in younger adults. Supporting tissues are weaker and less elastic and therefore provide less protection. This makes the elderly more liable to the complication of haematoma formation. Manipulation of the wound increases the risk of haematoma formation.   **91, 140**

The site of the wound on the leg also predisposes to haematoma as the venous pressure is increased when the leg is dependent.

2   The presence of haematoma increases the risk of infection. It also impairs the circulation to the skin which can cause necrosis.   **91, 103, 105**

3   Three weeks after such an injury in a younger patient you would expect to see capillary ingrowth and re-epithelisation. In the elderly there would be slower healing and less organisation. Macrophages will still be present with poor orientation of collagen fibrils and poor ingrowth of capillaries.   **93, 98, 99, 107**

1   The chances of healing occurring will be improved if the patient does not stand or walk on the affected leg for the first week, and keeps the leg elevated when sitting to promote venous drainage. She will need help with shopping. The use of bandages and dressings will make it difficult for her to bath. She may need help with this for a short period and it would be ideal if she could stay with a fit friend or relative until the wound heals.   **144, 145**

2   a) The advantage of treatment being carried out in the accident and emergency department is that medical staff are more easily available, to pick up the onset of complications at an early stage. Visits to the accident and emergency department may be difficult to arrange, may require an ambulance and may involve the patient waiting for long periods to be seen. Different nurses may be involved in the patient's care from day to day. They may not all appreciate all the particular factors involved in the care of this patient.   **147, 148**

b) The advantage of having the community nurse look after this patient is that she can be treated at home. The community nurse works on her own, and may not be able to refer the patient easily should complications arise. There are limitations on the range of materials and bandages available to the community nurse.

Patient's History

Joan Williams

Management of a major traumatic wound

Joan Williams is a 46 year old secretary. She is divorced and lives alone in a fourth floor flat with no lift. Her two daughters live nearby. Out shopping with one of her daughters, she stepped off the pavement and was knocked over by a bus. The wheels of the bus ran over her left leg. She remained fully conscious throughout, and has now been brought to the accident and emergency department by ambulance. You are the casualty officer. The appearance of the left lower limb is shown in the photograph. On the left, the tyre mark from the bus wheel can be clearly seen on the thigh. The photograph on the right shows the appearance after all the devitalised undermined skin has been removed under general anaesthetic.

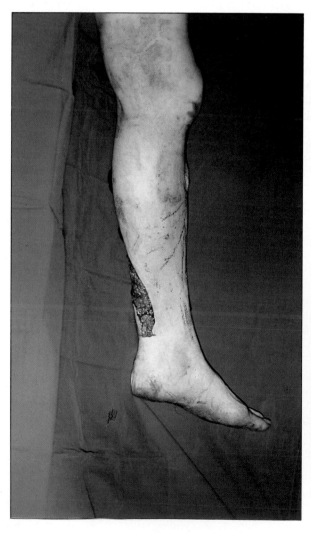

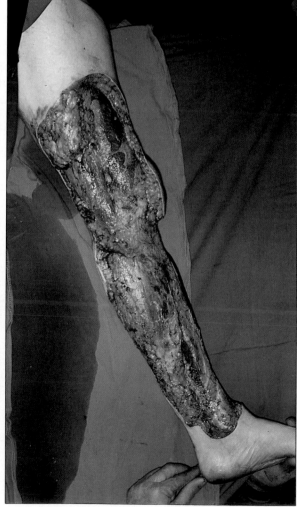

Patient Management Challenge - 6

Solve the problems with the help of your resource book

1	What are your priorities in managing this patient?	159
2	What term is used to describe this type of injury?	116
3	Assessment indicates no other serious injury. Radiographs have shown no fractures are present. When Mrs Williams is taken to theatre, what should be done?	160, 161, 162
4	What other measures, taken now, will diminish the likelihood of infections?	161, 172
1	How could you obtain epithelial cover of these wounds?	162
1	Why, in the future, might Mrs Williams' ankles become swollen?	141
2	In the left leg you can see muscle groups at the base of the wound. Why do you think separation of subcutaneous tissue from muscle has occurred?	116
1	Why is removal of all necrotic material and foreign bodies important in this case?	114, 160, 161
1	What problems is Mrs Williams likely to face on her return home?	145, 146, 148

Specialists' views on pages 40 - 41

Specialists' Views

Joan Williams

Related information can be found in Part C

1 The first priority here is to carry out general resuscitative measures, including fluid replacement. This patient may require a blood transfusion because of the extent of the injury. The amount of fluid replaced depends on time after injury and on the surface area of wound. Pain relief and full assessment of the patient for other serious injuries must also be addressed. A temporary wound dressing should be put in place to prevent desiccation and ease pain. Saline soaks are useful as temporary cover for exposed soft tissue and reduce the risk of contamination of open wounds. The patient requires admission to hospital. Once other serious life-threatening injuries have been excluded, you can concentrate your attention on her leg wounds.

159

2 The patient has sustained a major degloving injury.

116

3 The first aim is to prevent infection arising in the damaged area. Cleansing and thorough debriding of the wound should be carried out in theatre under a general anaesthetic as shown in the photograph on the right. The key point in managing any wound involving a large area is to obtain skin cover as quickly as possible, to prevent infection and tissue desiccation leading to further necrosis. This will help avoid complications developing as a result of joint immobility. The most appropriate approach in Mrs Williams' case is to skin graft the wounds.

160, 161, 162

4 There is a high risk of these wounds becoming infected. Meticulous attention to cleansing and surgical debridement is required as above. You should start the patient on prophylactic antibiotics immediately and also administer anti-tetanus therapy.

161, 172

1 Various types of skin grafts could be used. The treatment of choice is to excise underperfused skin flaps and remove the underlying fat. The skin can then be applied as a free graft, preferably meshed to enhance the take and avoid haematoma. If this skin is not available split skin grafts can be used. Cultured skin and skin substitutes are still experimental. Alternative sources of temporary cover are pig skin, related donor skin and combinations of autografts and allografts. Microvascular flaps may sometimes be used if bone or joints are exposed.

162

1 Destruction of superficial veins and lymphatics has occurred. These are important mechanisms to drain fluid from the limb.

141

2 Muscle groups are covered by fascia, which holds them together. It forms a natural plane of separation in such injuries because the fat is loosely attached to the fascia.

116

1 Risks of infection are increased dramatically in any wound that has necrotic or foreign material remaining.

114, 160, 161

1 This patient has been involved in a major traumatic incident which will influence the rest of her life. She may face a variety of psychological problems - from an understandable anxiety state to severe agoraphobia. She is almost certain to be left with some physical deficit, eg difficulty walking and extensive severe scarring. She should be able to return to work but will have difficulty disguising the severe scarring. This will limit her choice of clothing. Her current housing situation may limit her mobility and rehousing may be necessary.

145, 146, 148

41

Patient's History

Chris Johnston is a 55 year old baker. He is married with three children. He developed Crohn's disease three years ago, which settled on intensive medical treatment. Two weeks ago he returned to the out-patient clinic with a recurrence of abdominal pain and diarrhoea. He was prescribed steroids. However, his pain later increased and he was admitted as an emergency. He was dehydrated and had signs of peritonitis. Investigations confirmed the diagnosis of peritonitis. They also revealed anaemia and hypoproteinaemia. At operation, the perforated ileum was resected and a temporary ileostomy performed. A drain was brought out through a separate stab wound, as shown on the left.

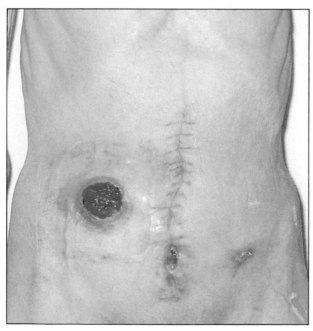

Double-barrelled ileo-colostomy with midline incision and drain site in abdomen.

42

Patient Management Challenge - 7

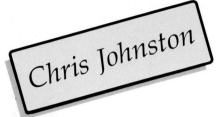

Solve the problems with the help of your resource book

	1	What immediate (48 hours post-operative) problems related to his wounds might complicate Mr Johnston's recovery?	113
	2	What factors will influence the timing of abdominal suture removal?	136
	3	What skin problems are associated with ileostomy effluent in the immediate post-operative period?	
	1	What factors influence the choice of sutures for the midline wound?	162
	2	What factors increase the risk of post-operative wound infection in Mr Johnston's case?	113, 172
	3	What steps may be taken to reduce the likelihood of bacterial contamination?	172
	1	What structures in the skin did the surgeon cut through making the midline abdominal and stoma wounds shown in the photographs?	82
	2	Why are the incisions made in these particular positions?	84
	1	What is the potential for infection in this type of operation?	113
	2	What are the likely infecting organisms?	104, 172
	1	List five aspects of this patient's life that may cause him anxiety in the future.	167
	2	After Mr Johnston leaves hospital, who can help him with the stoma?	148, 150, 154, 167

Specialists' views on pages 44 - 46

43

Specialists' Views

1 It is important to remember this patient has three wounds: an abdominal wound, a drain site and the wound around the stoma. Pain and haematoma formation associated with the wounds may complicate Mr Johnston's recovery. Careful handling of all tissues at the time of operation will reduce the likelihood of haematoma formation. The function and vascularity of the stoma may also cause concern.

    113

2 Factors influencing the timing of suture removal are blood supply to the area, the tension and movement to which the wound is subjected, the age and condition of the patient, cosmetic factors, underlying diagnosis, nutritional status of the patient, steroid therapy and the presence of wound complications. Sutures are generally removed from abdominal wounds about 10 days after the operation. In Mr Johnston's case, his pre-operative condition was poor, with weight loss, anaemia and hypoproteinaemia. Wound healing is therefore impaired and sutures are required to support the wound for longer, eg about 14 days or more, to reduce the risk of dehiscence.

    136

3 In the immediate post-operative period, the ileostomy effluent is a high volume (up to two litres per day) light green liquid. It contains enzymatic activity which will cause skin excoriation unless an effective skin barrier and ostomy pouch is worn.

1 The linea alba should be closed with either interrupted or continuous monofilament non-absorbable sutures placed at least 2-3 cm lateral to each side of the wound. The skin is closed with interrupted full thickness sutures. This prevents dehiscence of the wound.

    162

2 Mr Johnston's debilitated condition pre-operatively, and the fact that bowel preparation was impossible before surgery, make post-operative wound infection more likely. The urgent nature of the operation, in this case a perforated bowel, makes wound infection likely in 25% of patients, in contrast to planned surgery in a well prepared patient.

    113, 172

3 Appropriate antibiotics, given pre-operatively and peri-operatively, will help to reduce bacterial contamination. Skilful handling of the tissues at surgery will also reduce bacterial contamination. The drain should be sited well away from the main incision, to reduce the likelihood of infecting the main wound.

    172

1 The vertical abdominal incision cut through

- skin, both epidermis and dermis
- subcutaneous tissue
- linea alba
- peritoneum.

The stoma incision cut through

- skin
- subcutaneous tissue
- external and internal oblique and transversus muscles
- peritoneum.

82

2 The vertical incision allows easier and better access to the abdominal cavity, especially when the site of the perforation is unknown. In the midline, it lies along Langers' lines. In patients where cosmetic appearance and quality of healing is important, the choice of incision should follow anatomical lines. The midline contains fewer feeder blood vessels and bleeds less. Nerve supply to skin remains intact after healing.

84

The stoma incision is placed lateral to the rectus muscle, on the flattest area away from bony prominences to facilitate attachment of the stoma bag.

The incision for the drain is normally made away from the main wound, to reduce the likelihood of infecting the main wound.

1 Infection from bowel bacterial flora is a potential problem. Mr Johnston's general condition, removal of part of the bowel through an abdominal wound and the creation of a stoma all increase the risk of infective complications. This man falls into the highest risk category for wound infection, as his wound was contaminated at operation by the perforated bowel.

113

2 All bowel organisms especially E coli and the anaerobes, such as Bacteroides fragilis, are potential infecting organisms.

104, 172

1 Anxieties that stoma patients may experience include

i) work
There is no reason why this patient should not be able to return to work. Maintaining assiduous cleanliness of his hands will make his return to work as a baker feasible.

ii) sport and leisure
There is no reason why Mr Johnston should not take part in sport, for example swimming, or leisure activities, such as digging the garden, after the initial post-operative recovery phase.

iii) sexual activities
Mr Johnston's surgery should not prevent his returning to a normal sex life. It is important to appreciate that some relationships and marriages can suffer from anxieties created by a stoma even leading, in a few cases, to marital breakup. Education and possibly counselling of partner(s) may be necessary.

iv) mixing with others
Ileostomy patients may worry about:
- leakage from the stoma appliance
- the visibility of the stoma bag through clothing
- the effect of the stoma bag on their choice of clothing
- upleasant odour from the ileostomy.

The stoma therapist and Ileostomy Association will reassure patients and provide advice about such anxieties.

v) eating certain foods
Mr Johnston may worry that his diet will be restricted by the effects of certain foods on the functioning of his stoma. Some foods, particularly onions, peas and beans, may cause loose ileostomy diarrhoea with flatulence and odour. In the UK the stoma therapist and Ileostomy Association will provide helpful advice on this topic, too.

2 The general practitioner, community nurse, stoma therapist and patient associations such as the Ileostomy Association are often helpful. Patients with permanent ileostomies are entitled to free prescriptions. Patients can obtain appliances from major chemists.

167

148, 150, 154, 167

Patient's History

Accidental burns to hands

Jason Dixon, 28 years old, plays keyboards in a band. He is also a motor-bike enthusiast, doing all maintenance and repair work. Jason went out for lunch with other members of the band to celebrate signing a recording contract. He had a few alcoholic drinks. On return home he decided to work on his bike in the garage. It was cold and so he lit a calor gas heater. Because it was too close to the bike's petrol tank, the petrol fumes ignited, and there was a small explosion, burning Jason's face, hands and upper chest. He was able to call 999, and an ambulance brought him to the accident and emergency department of a large hospital. The facial and chest burns are superficial, but the appearance of Jason's hands, shown in the photographs, caused concern. The photographs were taken four days after the injury occurred. During this time the hands were treated in hand bags.

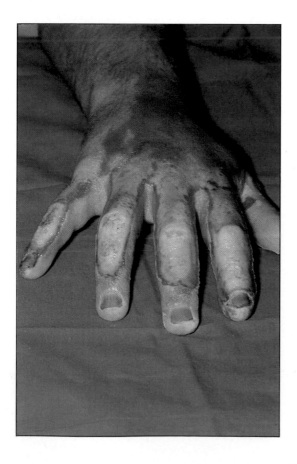
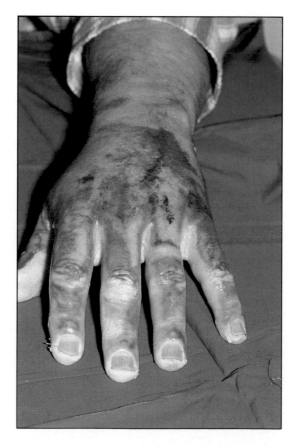

Jason Dixon

Solve the problems with the help of your resource book

1	Describe the appearance of the burns on Jason's hands.	135, 139, 140
2	What are the different steps involved in the management of any patient's wound?	149
3	Go through each of these steps for Jason's hand wounds.	10, 77, 146, 147, 149, 159, 160, 164, 170
4	List all the different groups of health care professionals and workers Jason may meet from the time of his burn.	147
5	List the other groups of health care professionals and workers who may be involved in Jason's care but whom he will not meet face-to-face.	

1	What effect will skin loss have on the underlying extensor tendons?	
2	How might damage to extensor tendons affect the right hand's function?	

1	What is the nature of the damage to the tissues at a cellular level?	117
2	Describe the pathological processes you would expect to see on the back of the fingers of Jason's right hand, if untreated	
	a) on day 1	94
	b) on day 3	95, 96
	c) on day 14	140

1	Will Jason be able to return to work? What factors will influence this?	146, 173

Specialists' views on pages 50 - 53

Specialists' Views

Jason Dixon

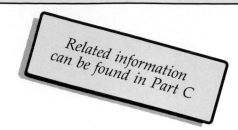

Related information can be found in Part C

1 Your description should include information on size and depth, shape, state, stage and site.   **135, 139, 140**

    Size   The palm and the back of the hand each represent 1% of the body surface. Jason's hand burns represent approximately 2½% of body surface area.

    Depth   The burned surface varies in colour from red to white to yellow over the right hand. This indicates that the burns are of variable depth. (The pink area suggests superficial burns.) The red areas over the dorsum of the right hand indicate a superficial partial thickness burn; the white area over the fingers signifies full thickness damage from which slough has separated by autolysis; the yellow area still has adherent slough and a deep dermal or full thickness burn.

    Shape   This burn is diffuse agreeing with the history of a flash burn.

    State   The heat of the burn kills skin and its commensal organisms alike. Initially a burn wound is sterile. However, recolonisation rapidly occurs and, if there is bacterial contamination, infection can supervene.

    Stage   It is a four day old burn. Inflammatory changes are underway and fluid is being lost from the damaged areas. Oedema is subsiding and some autolysis is taking place.

    Site   These burns involve the dorsal surfaces of both hands. In areas of full thickness damage, the degree of involvement of underlying structures cannot be assessed by inspection through the slough. In the fingers, skin overlies tendon with little subcutaneous fat. Therefore full thickness destruction of skin in this site can result in exposure and damage to underlying tendons.

2 The management of any wound requires assessment of both patient and wound (Organiser factors), formulation of a treatment plan, implementation of the plan with monitoring and, where appropriate, modification.   **149**

3 *Assessment* The Organiser should be used to assess all relevant factors. The **site**, in the hands, has implications for future function. Rapid healing is crucial to preserve maximum mobility. At this **stage**, the wounds will be very painful and Jason requires appropriate and regular analgesia. Lines of demarcation of dead tissue are now more clearly defined and the surgeon can see what tissue must be removed.   **10, 77, 159**

The **cause**, thermal injury, results in surface damage. Deep damage to underlying structures implies prolonged exposure, very high temperature or electrical burn. Prolonged exposure generally implies impaired consciousness, e.g. alcohol or drug abuse, epilepsy, coma, or self-wounding. The **form** has been detailed in the answer to Question 1. The **environment**, in which he is to be managed, will be determined by his need for **carers** and by the degree of specialised care required. The **health care** system in the UK provides specialised facilities for the care of burns.

Formulation of a treatment plan

Treatment of Jason's hand wounds can be considered in three phases: immediate, intermediate and long-term. Remember we are considering only his hand wounds and not the additional measures which will be required for his other wounds.

149

Immediate treatment includes

- analgesia
- explanation of the injury and immediate management to the patient
- swabbing the wound for bacteriology
- cleansing the wound
- protection of the wound by a dressing
- admission to the regional burns unit (RBU)
- elevation of hands to reduce oedema.

147, 160, 164, 170

Intermediate treatment involves

- definitive treatment of the wound, which in this case is surgical excision and cover using a skin flap because the extensor tendons were exposed after surgical excision of the burn slough. Here, the skin flap was taken from Jason's groin.
- subsequent physiotherapy to maintain hand function

146, 162

Long-term management entails:

- continuing physiotherapy
- occupational therapy
- additional surgical procedures
- employment counselling/retraining.

146

Implementation of treatment plan

- implementation starts in casualty with assessment and administration of analgesia
- is continued by admission to the RBU, where expertise and specialised facilities are available
- is maintained in the community with measures to maximise Jason's hand function and provide support as the extent of his disability is revealed.

Monitoring and modification

Monitoring should be regular and modifications made, as necessary. Both will depend on the individual case.

4 It is evident that many different health care professionals are involved in the management of such an injury. Liaison and good communication between the different groups is essential.

Health care professionals Jason may meet include

- ambulance team
- accident and emergency receptionist and nursing staff
- casualty officer
- house officer in RBU (regional burns unit)
- porters
- specialist nursing and medical staff in RBU
- receptionist in RBU
- phlebotomist
- domestics and other lay support workers
- dietician
- physiotherapist
- medical photographer
- anaesthetist
- theatre staff
- radiographer
- clinical pharmacist
- occupational therapist
- clinical psychologist
- orthotist
- pressure garment maker
- medical social worker
- community nurse
- general practitioner and primary health care team
- out-patient staff in burns clinic physiotherapy department, occupational therapy and orthotics
- rehabilitation medicine staff.

5 Health care professionals Jason will not meet include:

- ambulance control and hospital switchboard
- laboratory staff in haematology, blood transfusion, bacteriology and biochemistry
- pharmacy staff
- catering, laundry, secretarial, administrative and medical records staff
- theatre sterile supply unit workers
- radiologist and radiology staff

1 Extensor tendons lie directly under the skin on the dorsum of the fingers. Skin loss breaches the skin's protective barrier in this site leading to exposure of tendons. Exposure produces desiccation of the fragile paratenon and tendon itself. Both may die as a result.

2 Loss of extensor tendon function results in inability to straighten the fingers. Unopposed flexor tendon action bends the fingers causing a flexion contracture, (bouttoniere deformity).

1 Heat causes tissue damage by coagulating protein.   **117**

2   a) Day 1
     Tissue damage triggers inflammation, with capillary
     dilatation, increased permeability of blood vessels
     and leakage of plasma. Heat coagulation of enzymes   **94**
     reduces autolysis.

     b) Day 3
     Macrophages and polymorphs have been attracted
     into the area by chemotaxis. These cells phagocytose   **95, 96**
     dead tissue, starting the natural debridement process
     of autolysis.

     c) Day 14
     Autolysis will begin to separate necrotic tissue from
     viable tissue. Necrotic tissue will eventually be shed   **140**
     as slough. The presence of necrotic tissue in the
     wound increases the potential for infection. Most
     untreated burns would show clear evidence of infection
     by this stage.

1 Jason's ability to play a keyboard again will depend on   **146 173**
     mobility after surgery. Equally important are his own
     motivation and perseverance with physiotherapy over many
     months. It is by no means certain that he will fully regain his
     keyboard ability.

Patient's History

Alastair Jackson

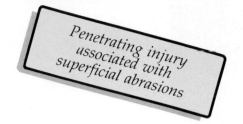

Penetrating injury ussociated with superficial abrasions

Alastair Jackson is 18 years old and has worked as a supermarket shelf-filler for 21 months. He lives with his parents. When riding his bike to work Alastair crashed into the back of a car and fell off, sustaining multiple grazes to his cheek, nose and both hands. He also sustained a cut from a small piece of glass, at the base of his right index finger. The cut was sutured in a nearby cottage hospital. Two days later, he removed the dressing. He found he could not flex the end of his index finger and it felt numb. He consulted his doctor the following day. She obtained an urgent out-patient appointment with a hand surgeon at the hospital. The appearance of his hand is shown on the photograph on the left. The surgeon arranged for Alastair's admission for surgery. Alastair spent 72 hours in hospital and was discharged home in a splint. Regular out-patient review and physiotherapy followed.

You have been asked to assist the hand surgeon in his clinic when Alastair returns for one of his regular follow-up appointments. It is now eight weeks since his surgery. He is generally pleased with the progress his hand is making and is working well with the physiotherapist. However, he is worried today about the appearance of his face. His cheek looks as if it has a dirty mark, and acquaintances are commenting on this.

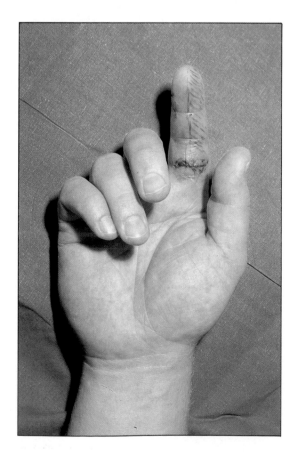

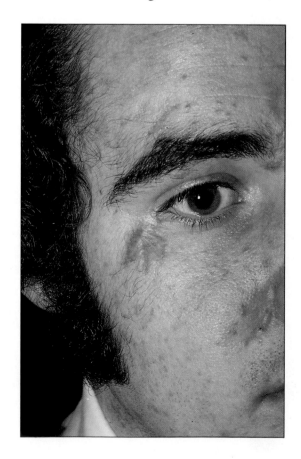

Solve the problems with the help of your resource book

1	What do you think has caused the 'dirty mark' on Alastair's face?	160
2	How can this 'dirty mark' be treated now?	160
3	What advice would Alastair have been given about the position of his hand and arm when he was discharged after surgery?	146
4	If Alastair had returned to the hospital four days after his surgery, complaining of increased pain under the dressing, what would you have done?	170
5	What surgery has Alastair undergone?	

1	Which muscle is responsible for flexion of the terminal phalanx of a finger?	
2	How many tendons run on the palmar surface of the fingers:	
	a) at the proximal interphalangeal joint?	
	b) at the distal interphalangeal joint?	
3	What other important structures were at risk from this hand injury?	
4	What does the blue shading on Alastair's finger indicate?	86

1	How has the healing of Alastair's hand laceration differed from that of his facial abrasions?	83, 93

1	Alastair is likely to be off work for several weeks. What financial benefits might be available to him?	145
2	The nearest physiotherapy department is half an hour away by bus. Alastair cannot afford the fare. What can be done about this?	145

Specialists' views on pages 56 - 57

Specialists' Views

Alastair Jackson

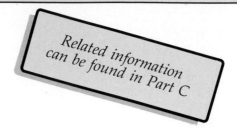

Related information can be found in Part C

1 The "dirty mark" on Alastair's face is a complication of healing called traumatic tattooing. It is caused by inadequate cleansing of a wound which then heals with persistent foreign material within the tissue. — **160**

2 Traumatic tattooing can only be treated surgically. In this case, as a small area is involved, dermabrasion would be tried. If the pigment were deep, excision would be required. — **160**

3 On discharge from hospital, Alastair would have been advised to maintain the hand in an elevated position in a sling. This position encourages drainage from the hand and arm, preventing oedema. He would also have been advised to remove the hand from the sling at least three times a day, to exercise the elbow and shoulder, thereby preventing joint stiffness. — **146**

4 Had Alastair returned complaining of pain, the wound dressings and splint would have been carefully removed. The wound would then have been inspected, to exclude complications such as haematoma or infection. If the dressing or appliance is too tight, the hand may become oedematous and this also results in pain. — **170**

5 Delayed primary repair of the damaged tendon and repair of digital nerve injury has been carried out.

1 The muscle responsible for flexion of the terminal phalanx of the finger is the flexor digitorum profundus.

2 a) There are three tendons at the level of the proximal interphalangeal joint. These are the two slips of the flexor digitorum superficialis and the flexor digitorum profundus tendon.

   b) At the distal interphalangeal joint there is only one tendon - the flexor digitorum profundus.

3 Alastair injured only the central digitorum profundus tendon and the radial digital nerve. Also at risk were the flexor digitorum superficialis tendons plus the ulnar digital nerves and ulnar and radial digital blood vessels.

4 This is the area of absent sensation caused by damage to the radial digital nerve. — **86**

1 The facial abrasions have healed by regeneration of the epithelium from the basal layer of the skin remaining in the wound. The lacerations of the hand healed by primary intention, as the edges were sutured close together. — **83, 93**

1 Depending on the society the patient lives in, financial support may be available. In the UK, Alastair will be eligible for sickness benefit as he has been employed for a sufficient length of time and he will have paid National Insurance. He will be unable to claim any extra financial support as he is living at home. He will not be entitled to compensation, unless he had private insurance cover. His ability to return to work is unlikely to be affected in his present occupation, but it may be important in other types of work. If he had been permanently disabled, a disability pension may have been payable.

145

2 Physiotherapy is essential to ensure proper recovery. It is important to give Alastair exercises to undertake at home and that he attends the local physiotherapy department. The provision of an ambulance to transport him to hospital cannot be justified. Refund of public transport expenses for travel to hospital is possible, but many patients are not aware of this. The hospital social worker will provide full details.

145

Patient's History

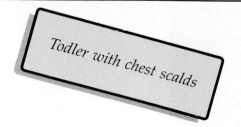

A newly qualified general practitioner, you are phoned by the mother of an active one year old toddler, Alice O'Connor. Alice lives with her mother, a single parent, in bed and breakfast accommodation while awaiting housing from the local council. Her mother is very distressed and reports that Alice had fallen into a bath of scalding water. This happened because hot water had been put in first. When Alice's mother heard the screams she pulled Alice out and splashed cold water from the basin over the burn. You advise the mother that she should take Alice immediately to hospital, where she is admitted for treatment. Her appearance is shown in the photograph.

Five weeks later, the mother comes to see you with Alice. Dressings are no longer required for the burn wounds. The mother is, however, very concerned about the present appearance of the scars and the number of problems Alice seems to have in returning to her usual cheerful self.

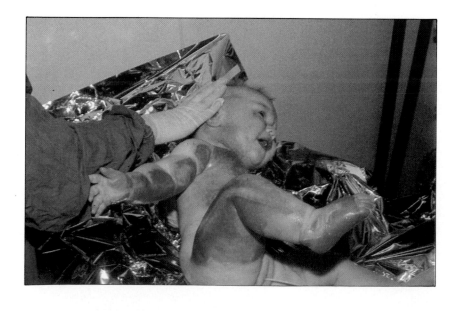

Alice O'Connor

Solve the problems with the help of your resource book

1	At the time of the accident, when you speak to Alice's mother on the telephone, what information do you need from her?	112
2	What measures would you advise the mother to take?	149
3	What information can be obtained from examining the burns?	117, 118, 139
4	What complications can be expected, as Alice grows into a young woman? What treatment might be required?	98, 101, 118
5	What rare complications can occur in burn scars later in life?	129

1	Burns are classified into three groups. What are they? What layers and which structures would you expect to be damaged in each type of burn?	82, 118
2	What characteristics of skin allow for full joint mobility?	84

1	Why does a large burn result in a massive amount of fluid loss?	94, 95
2	What bacteria might you expect to grow from a wound swab of an uninfected granulating burn wound?	104, 167
3	Why do some areas of a burn heal with no permanent scar, while other areas leave scarring?	83, 84
4	What is a hypertrophic scar and how does it differ from normal and keloid scarring?	101, 102

1	What problems may arise when Alice attends school?	119, 145
2	What measures could you take to ease the situation for Alice?	119
3	Whose help can you enlist to support Alice and her mother in the community?	119, 150

Specialists' views on pages 60 - 62

Specialists' Views

Alice O'Connor

Related information can be found in Part C

1 When speaking to Alice's mother, you should find out **when** the accident occurred. Fluid loss begins soon after the accident. It is important to know approximately how much fluid has been lost in the time between the accident and attaining medical care. The **cause** of the accident, in this case, scalding with hot liquid, may give you a clue to the depth of damage. Similarly, any first aid measures taken may influence the depth of damage. The **age** of the child will also be required. The extent of the injury is vital information to enable you to decide if hospital referral is necessary. If the burn covers more than 8% of the child's body surface urgent hospital treatment is essential as intravenous fluid replacement to prevent shock is required.

112

2 The mother should be advised to remove any clothing, because this tends to hold hot liquid against the child's skin. Cold water should be applied to the scald to drop skin termperature. This can be achieved by immersing the child in a shower/bath or by laying wet towels on the area. However, it is important that the child should not become chilled and unscalded areas should be wrapped up well.

149

3 When examining the burn, it is important to estimate the size in terms of percentage surface area. Close examination of the burn may also give information as to the depth of damage. This is vital, to enable decisions to be made concerning the use of conservative measures or surgical treatment. The depth has significant influence on whether permanent scarring can be expected. If the history does not seem appropriate to the findings on examination, non-accidental causes of injury should be considered.

117, 118, 139

4 As Alice grows up, any tight scarring of the chest will be unsightly, may have psychological implications and may interfere with breast development. At puberty, it is important to monitor the situation closely so that scar release and grafting can be performed, should breast growth be impeded. A severe burn involving the nipple during childhood will prevent its development and preclude breast feeding.

98, 101, 118

5 Marjolin reported skin carcinoma arising in old scars. Scars in childhood have the potential for malignant transformation in later life but this is very rare.

129

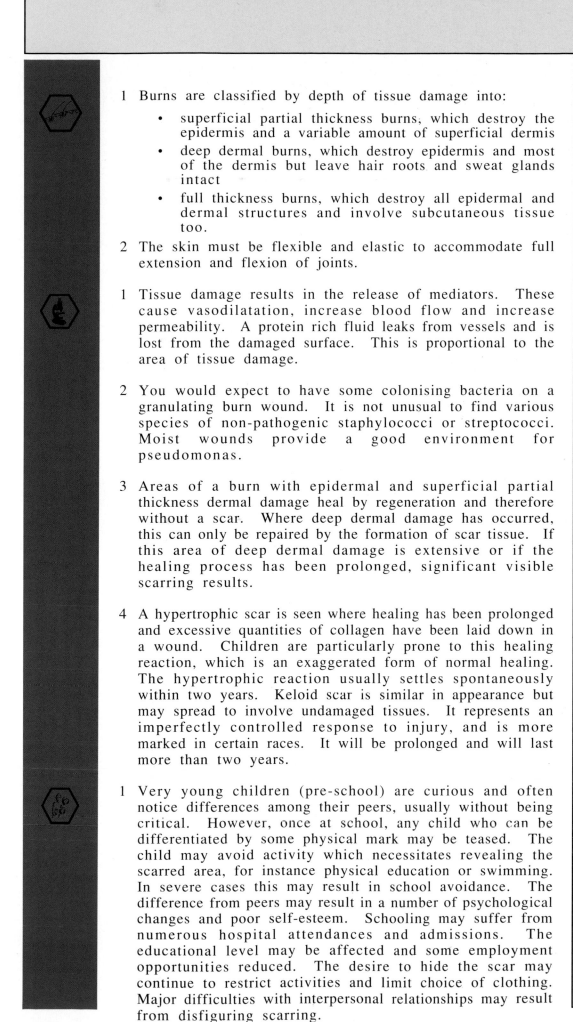

1 Burns are classified by depth of tissue damage into:

- superficial partial thickness burns, which destroy the epidermis and a variable amount of superficial dermis
- deep dermal burns, which destroy epidermis and most of the dermis but leave hair roots and sweat glands intact
- full thickness burns, which destroy all epidermal and dermal structures and involve subcutaneous tissue too.

82, 118

2 The skin must be flexible and elastic to accommodate full extension and flexion of joints.

84

1 Tissue damage results in the release of mediators. These cause vasodilatation, increase blood flow and increase permeability. A protein rich fluid leaks from vessels and is lost from the damaged surface. This is proportional to the area of tissue damage.

94, 95

2 You would expect to have some colonising bacteria on a granulating burn wound. It is not unusual to find various species of non-pathogenic staphylococci or streptococci. Moist wounds provide a good environment for pseudomonas.

104, 167

3 Areas of a burn with epidermal and superficial partial thickness dermal damage heal by regeneration and therefore without a scar. Where deep dermal damage has occurred, this can only be repaired by the formation of scar tissue. If this area of deep dermal damage is extensive or if the healing process has been prolonged, significant visible scarring results.

83, 84

4 A hypertrophic scar is seen where healing has been prolonged and excessive quantities of collagen have been laid down in a wound. Children are particularly prone to this healing reaction, which is an exaggerated form of normal healing. The hypertrophic reaction usually settles spontaneously within two years. Keloid scar is similar in appearance but may spread to involve undamaged tissues. It represents an imperfectly controlled response to injury, and is more marked in certain races. It will be prolonged and will last more than two years.

101, 102

1 Very young children (pre-school) are curious and often notice differences among their peers, usually without being critical. However, once at school, any child who can be differentiated by some physical mark may be teased. The child may avoid activity which necessitates revealing the scarred area, for instance physical education or swimming. In severe cases this may result in school avoidance. The difference from peers may result in a number of psychological changes and poor self-esteem. Schooling may suffer from numerous hospital attendances and admissions. The educational level may be affected and some employment opportunities reduced. The desire to hide the scar may continue to restrict activities and limit choice of clothing. Major difficulties with interpersonal relationships may result from disfiguring scarring.

119, 145

61

2 A sensible choice of clothing to disguise obvious scarring may help. Children who have difficulties coping with school may be seen with their parents, by an educational psychologist. Close liaison is required with school teachers, to explain the problems the child is experiencing. Specialist advice about the management of scarring should be sought. The hospital should try to arrange any admissions during school holidays.

119

3 A health visitor and you, the general practitioner are the most likely first point of contact in the community. Nursery attendance now will encourage her to mix successfully with other children before she reaches school age. The clinical medical officer in the health authority clinic may well monitor Alice's general development. Child psychologists and psychiatrists may be introduced if behavioural difficulties occur. Social workers may assist with housing difficulties and any special clothing required. Burn support groups can offer encouragement and assistance to the parent and child. Support from local Gingerbread groups for single parents may be available.

119, 150

Patient's History

Arthur Baker

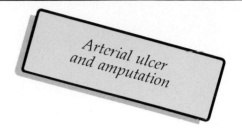

Arterial ulcer and amputation

Arthur Baker is a 55 year old unemployed labourer, who has smoked heavily for the past 40 years. He had to give up work six months ago, after developing pain in his legs on walking. The pain has eased since he stopped work, but his weight has increased. His chronic obstructive airways disease has deteriorated in recent weeks. He lives in a two bedroomed council house with his wife who works as a part-time cleaner.

Mr Baker presented with the foot ulcer shown on the left and was referred to hospital. Reconstructive surgery was carried out on his leg. Although initially there was an improvement in the condition of his leg, the graft clotted and did not give a satisfactory result. Mr Baker underwent amputation and the resulting stump is shown on the right.

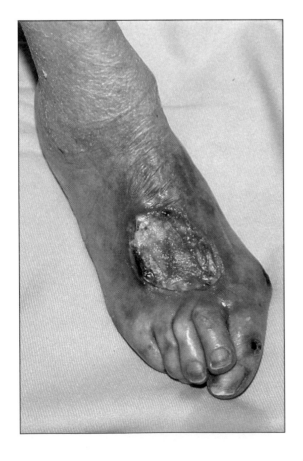

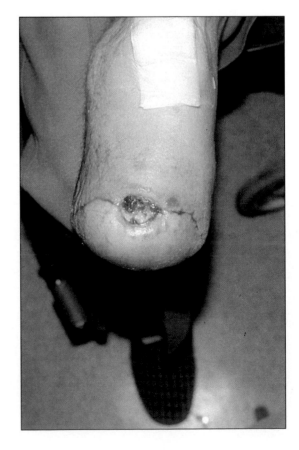

Solve the problems with the help of your resource book

1	If you were Arthur Baker's general practitioner, how would you dress the wound shown on the left? What other measures would you suggest while he is awaiting admission to hospital?	**103, 121, 171, 173**
2	Why is compression bandaging of a leg affected by peripheral vascular disease a potentially hazardous procedure?	**171**
3	How would you make a diagnosis of arterial leg ulceration?	**124**
4	How would you manage the stump wound shown on the right?	**169**
1	What happens in an exercising muscle if the oxygen supply is insufficient? What would the exercising person experience? What happens when exercise stops?	
2	How might a sympathectomy promote healing of Arthur's ulcer?	
3	The amputation stump in this patient must take over the weight bearing function normally performed by the sole of the foot. Make a list of how these two surfaces differ.	
1	What series of events leads to the appearance of an ulcerated area in a patient with arterial insufficiency?	**124**
2	What causes of ulceration should be excluded when making the diagnosis of arterial ulceration?	**121**
1	Arteriosclerosis and subsequent amputation are very much commoner in smokers. What advice would you give Arthur Baker about smoking? What measures are available to assist him stopping?	**121**
2	What complications of the amputation should the general practitioner or community nurse look for? What advice should Arthur Baker be given to prevent these occurring?	**121, 127, 150**

Specialists' views on pages 66 - 67

Arthur Baker

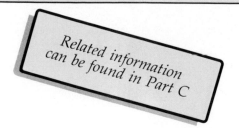

Related information can be found in Part C

1   The general practitioner will probably arrange for the practice nurse or the district nurse to dress the ulcer. The ulcer needs to be kept clean, free of necrotic tissue, and moist. It is important that the dressings are not constricting. He should be advised to wear loose, comfortable footwear. There is evidence of possible pressure related trauma on the medial side of the toes.

   Gentle regular exercise should be advised. This promotes the development of a collateral blood supply, which diminishes peripheral ischaemia. Smoking should be forbidden, to remove the vasoconstrictor action of nicotine and allow the collaterals to open up. A low fat diet, calorie controlled if appropriate, and stopping smoking will help limit disease progression.

103, 121, 171, 173

2   Compression bandaging applies external pressure to the leg. In patients with peripheral vascular disease this can lead to collapse of the underperfused capillary bed, as arterial pressures are lower than normal. Capillary bed collapse leads to anoxia and tissue death.

171

3   The patient's history may indicate that the underlying cause of ulceration is arterial insufficiency. Symptoms such as pain on walking (intermittent claudication), or rest pain at night are characteristic. On examination ulcers are commonly punched out, indolent and associated with signs of peripheral vascular disease such as cool hairless skin and reduced or absent peripheral pulses. A Doppler ultrasound examination with brachial ankle ratio will confirm arterial insufficiency. Other causes should be excluded, such as vasculitis, venous insufficiency, diabetes and rarer conditions, e.g. sickle cell disease.

124

4   The wound should be swabbed for bacteriological culture. A dressing which does not stick to the wound, such as a hydrocolloid, should be selected and changed as necessary. Weight bearing on this stump should be avoided until healing is complete.

169

1   Tissue with an oxygen supply inadequate for its activity converts to anaerobic metabolism. A build-up of lactic acid in exercising the muscle results in pain and later stiffness. Following exercise, lactic acid is oxidised and the oxygen debt paid back.

2 A sympathectomy blocks the passage of impulses in sympathetic nerves to blood vessels. This leads to vasodilation of the vascular bed of the skin. Healing of the skin may be improved.

3 The surface of the foot and that of the stump differ in:
- surface area,
- nature of underlying bony structures,
- skin thickness,
- presence of a scar,
- general cushioning nature of the soft tissues
- attachment to soft tissues to bone.

Shearing, localised pressure points and insensate scar all contribute to the formation of pressure sores.

1 Arterial ulcers may result from minor trauma, localised pressure, or a minor skin infection. Inflammation leads to an increased metabolic demand for oxygen in the skin, which the vascular system is unable to meet. The tissues become hypoxic and this leads to cell death and skin breakdown.

124

2 The main differential diagnoses to be considered in ulceration of a lower limb are

121

- venous insufficiency,
- arterial insufficiency,
- vasculitis,
- pressure effects,
- diabetes.

Less frequently seen are ulceration due to sickle cell disease and tropical infections.

1 Smoking is a major risk factor. It can cause, and aggravate vascular disease and all patients should be advised to stop smoking. However, many have been heavy smokers since early adulthood and find stopping extremely difficult. You should provide as much detailed information as possible to improve motivation. Withdrawal symptoms may be reduced by provision of nicotine chewing gum. Some patients find hypnotherapy effective in reinforcing motivation and helping perseverance.

121

2 Carers in the community should be aware of the danger of pressure sores developing in non-ambulant patients and stump or calliper sores in the more mobile. It is important that amputees watch their weight, as decreased activity with unchanged diet may lead to obesity. This has implications for mobility and carries an increased risk of pressure sores. Where a patient is at risk from pressure sores, appropriate provision should be made for the supply and maintenance of pressure relieving devices such as specialised wheelchair cushions or special mattress overlays. Callipers, wheelchairs and prostheses are individually prescribed. Growth, changes in lifestyle, or increasing weight may necessitate adjustments.

121, 127, 150

Patient's History

Maria Kordylewska

A wound which is unlikely to heal

Maria Kordylewska is a 69 year old unmarried woman. She is illiterate and of low IQ, but has managed to live at home without being institutionalised. She now lives in sheltered housing. The home help was concerned about the odour in the patient's home and Maria finally confided in the home help about 'the area of exzema' on her left breast, shown in the photograph. The home help contacted the general practitioner, who arranged her admission to hospital as an emergency. On examination, she was found to have an ulcerating foul-smelling breast wound overlying a large breast cancer. She had visibly enlarged left supraclavicular lymph nodes but metastatic screening tests for other spread (metastases) were otherwise negative. Histology of the wound and underlying mass confirmed the presence of invasive intraduct carcinoma of the breast.

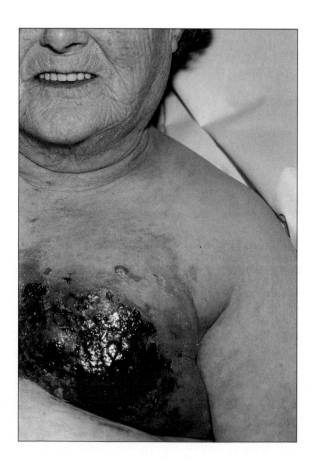

Solve the problems with the help of your resource book

1   How would you dress this wound?   167

2   How would you manage the pain associated with   170
     dressing this wound?

1   What might enable healing of the skin lesion to take
     place?

1   What prevents normal epithelial healing in this
     patient's wound?

2   What causes the odour?   167

1   How should the wound be managed, once Maria   167, 169
     returns home?

2   What other problems, related to the wound, is she   150
     likely to have?

3   How would you deal with her psychological reaction
     to her condition?

Specialists' views on page 70

Maria Kordylewska

Related information can be found in Part C

1 The wound should be dressed frequently with, for example, an odour-absorbing charcoal-impregnated dressing to control the smell and absorb any discharge.   **167**

2 Initially, dressing changes may be painful and a small intravenous injection of 2-3 milligrams of morphine might be required beforehand. As the pain diminishes, one of the non-steroidal anti-inflammatory group of drugs, such as ibuprofen, would be useful to control it.   **170**

1 Chemotherapy might help. Maria was given tamoxifen 40 milligrams per day to shrink the growth and reduce the discharge. Culture of the tumour confirmed it was sensitive to this chemotherapeutic agent. Although reduction in tumour size may be achieved, it is unlikely that epithelial healing will ever take place.

1 Intraepidermal invasion of carcinoma prolongs the inflammatory phase of healing. This blocks the subsequent phases (proliferation and maturation).

2 It is thought that the odour is caused by gas produced by bacteria infecting necrotic tissue.   **167**

1 This wound is unlikely to heal and will probably have to be dressed for the rest of Maria's life. Unfortunately, odour-absorbing charcoal-impregnated dressings are not currently available in the community in the UK. When prescribing dressings their availability in the community should be borne in mind. Dressings which do not adhere, such as an alginate with secondary dressing or paraffin gauze, should be used, to minimise associated pain.   **167, 169**

2 The odour from the wound may increase her social isolation. She has a home help who continues to see her daily and visits from a Macmillan Nurse can be arranged. Eventual hospice admission is likely for Maria.   **150**

3 Maria is completely denying her problem. Since she is firmly committed to this reaction, it is unwise to force an understanding of the exact nature of her condition on her.

The Wound Programme

Part A   The Reader's Guide

Part B   Patient Management Challenges

Part C   What You Need to Know about Wounds

Part D   Glossary

Part E   Consensus Statement

The important facts and ideas you will need to apply when managing patients with wounds. The contents are on page 4

Section 1
A New Era in Wound Healing

This section highlights the importance of wound healing. In it we introduce an Organiser to help you assess wounds, particularly important in this period of change and development.

If you feel you
are familiar with
the contents of
Section 1, move
on to another
section

The Importance of Wound Healing

We illustrate how an understanding of wounds will be useful for you.

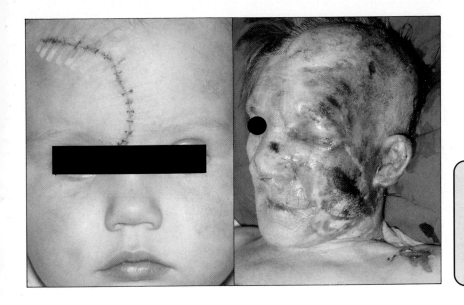

Wounds are an everyday occurrence affecting young and old, the healthy and the sick. Most health care professionals will be asked for advice about a wound.

Who manages wounds?

A general practitioner will treat any number of minor accidents, scalds, post-surgical wounds and long-standing ulcers. A nurse must understand wounds and how they are treated. A surgeon must appreciate the differences in healing which exist in different tissues. The theory of wound healing can then be translated into good clinical practice. A physician may be asked to treat chronic wounds.

What is healing?

Injury to any tissue initiates a complex series of responses. These responses help to clear damaged cells and other unwanted elements, to protect viable tissues and to reconstitute the area. The basic mechanisms are the same for all tissues. Variations occur according to the structure and function of the individual tissue. Bone produces callus when fractured. Muscle and skin form a fibrous scar.

Growth, healing and malignancy

The study of the control mechanisms of healing may shed light on the defects involved in oncogenesis. Development, growth and healing all involve a series of well co-ordinated cellular processes which results in new tissue formation. The malignant process is also one of new tissue formation but control is defective or absent: new tissue is produced irrespective of need.

A New Era in Wound Care

An understanding of recent developments in this expanding field will help you to evaluate changing practice.

"I dressed the wound. God healed it." Paracelsus (1493-1541)

Past, present and future

In the past the primary aim of treatment was to protect the wound while nature repaired the damage. Current practice has the additional aim of creating the ideal local climate for cells involved in healing. In the future, as knowledge of factors controlling healing increases, it may be possible to manipulate these factors to influence healing.

Climate 164

Research techniques

The development of new biological research techniques has led to great advances in our understanding of the way the healing process is controlled. Protein sequencing has assisted the isolation, identification and synthesis of controlling substances. New cell culture techniques have allowed the role of individual cell types to be better evaluated. Study of wounds has provided a better idea of the interrelationship of the various stimulating and inhibitory elements.

Substances 92
Cell types 99

Future research

Sufficiently large amounts of some of the newly identified wound substances can now be produced by the biotechnology industry to allow clinical trials to take place. As yet there is insufficient understanding of the balances and counterbalances that exist between these numerous factors in vivo. Considerable research efforts are currently focused on this area.

Classification and treatment of chronic non-healing wounds.
Knighton D R, Cicero K F, Fiegel V D, Austin L L and Butler E L.
Ann Surg 1986; **204**: 322-330.

The Wound Organiser

An Organiser for the study of wounds and for the assessment of patients with wounds.

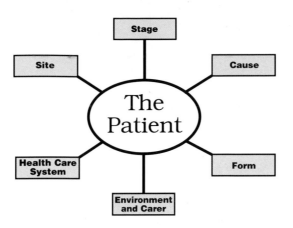

The Wound Organiser

Aspects of the Organiser

 When considering the management of a patient who has a wound, six aspects must be taken into account. The patient is the central consideration.

- site - tissue types involved and the anatomical position of the wound
- stage - how far the healing processes have progressed
- cause - the nature of the wound eg a burn, trauma, surgery
- form - the size, shape and state of the wound
- environment and carer - in home or hospital, self-care or nursed
- health care system - the organisation and availability of care.

The Wound Organiser can be applied when considering the management of a patient with damage to any tissue type. In this programme it is applied to the management of skin wounds. These are common, and skin healing has been extensively studied as access is easy and the clinical manifestations are available for inspection. Knowledge of healing in skin can provide a useful insight into the healing processes of other tissues and how they react to damaging disease processes, eg rheumatoid arthritis.

Integration

 Complete understanding of wound care requires knowledge from a wide range of disciplines. These include basic medical sciences, such as anatomy and physiology, the pathological sciences and clinical subjects, eg medicine and surgery. An understanding of the health care system, both in the hospital and community, and of the impact of wounds on the individual in society is also required. Using the Organiser can bring together all aspects of patient wound care in a logical and organised way.

The Wound Matrix. Harding K. In preparation.

Section 2
Site: Special Features of the Skin Relevant to Wounds

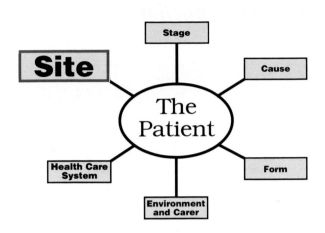

The Wound Organiser

Now that you understand why wound healing is important, consider the first aspect of the Wound Organiser - the site of the wound. Healing of skin wounds is influenced by the special features of skin, and differences between anatomical regions.

Look at the Guide to Section 2 on Page 8. If you are familiar with skin structure and function, move on to another section

Guide to Section 2

Site: Skin Structure and Function

Layer	Function	Effects of Wound
Epidermis **Epithelial cells** - arise from basal cell layer, shed as flattened anuclear squames. **Melanocytes** - neural crest cells producing melanin.	Barrier to injury, contamination and moisture loss. Protect against UV light; responsible for skin pigmentation and tanning.	Allows infection, water loss, and tissue desiccation. Patchy alteration in skin colour.
Dermis Collagen - protein; a major consitutent. Elastin - protein. Nerves Capillaries - dense network supplied from hypodermis.	Strength and support. Elasticity Detect pain, temperature, touch, position, vibration. Provide information on environment. Protection. Provide supply of nutrients and oxygen and remove waste products.	Strength of repair depends on amount and quality of collagen. Altered appearance. Reduced amount in scar tissue which is inelastic. Nerve damage causes loss of sensation leading to increased susceptibility to injury. Form major component of granulation tissue.
Epidermal appendages Hair follicles - lined by epidermal cells. Sweat glands. Sebaceous glands.	Produce hair: • insulation/thermoregulation increase sensititivy of skin especially to light touch. • physical appearance. Produce sweat: • thermoregulation. Produce sebum: • maintains hair and skin condition and pH. • antimicrobial.	Unaffected by superficial damage. Destroyed by full thickness damage, leading to hair loss. Source of epidermal cells in partial thickness wounds. Unaffected by superficial damage. Destroyed by full thickness damage leading to localised loss of sweat production. Unaffected by superficial damage. Destroyed by full thickness damage, leading to dry, fissured scar.
Hypodermis or subcutaneous tissue Fat - soft mobile layer. Connective tissue - contains nerve and blood supply.	Insulates, stores energy, cushions. Attaches skin to underlying tissue. Supports. Divides tissue into compartments.	Contour defects. Tethering of skin. Shearing interrupts nerve and blood supply.

The Significance of Wounds

Wounding affects the barrier and regulatory functions of the skin.

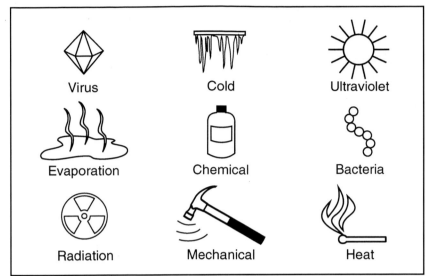

Hazards of the environment.

Virus — Cold — Ultraviolet — Evaporation — Chemical — Bacteria — Radiation — Mechanical — Heat

> "Tissue repair is a requisite sequel of cutaneous injury for the re-establishment of skin homoeostasis." R A F Clark

Skin as a barrier

 The skin acts as a barrier to environmental hazards. It protects against

- mechanical damage,
- desiccation,
- irradiation,
- thermal effects,
- invasion by micro-organisms.

Keratin is an intermediate filament protein in the outer layers of skin. It forms a waterproof covering and prevents excess water loss. Inert keratin and the antimicrobial properties of sebum help to deter bacterial invasion. Melanin is a polymeric, granular substance responsible for skin pigmentation. It acts as a defence against natural ultraviolet radiation.

Barrier breakdown

 Wounding leads to a breakdown in the protective function of skin. Bacteria gain entry to deeper tissues and may overcome the body's defence, giving rise to infection. When large areas of skin are damaged, as in a burn, the volume and nature of fluid lost from the wound surface may be life threatening. Remember that chemicals are more readily absorbed from damaged skin surfaces. This has important implications when applying cream, ointment or powder to wounds.

Sun and the wound

 The exposure of newly healed tissue to sunlight may induce redness, blistering or an increase in pigmentation of the area. Patients with large areas of newly healed tissue should be warned of the possibilities which can be unsightly.

Desiccation G

Keratin G
Sebum G
Invasion 104
Melanin G

Infection G
Burn 117

Chemicals 169

 Intermediate filaments. Steinert P M and Parry D A D. Annu Rev Cell Biol 1985; **1**: 41-65.

Layers of the Skin

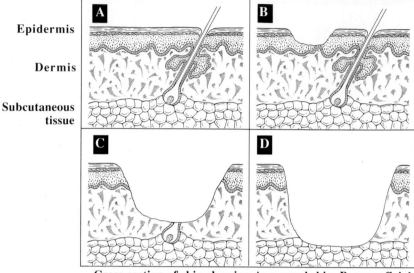

Epidermis

Dermis

Subcutaneous tissue

Cross section of skin showing A: normal skin, B: superficial wound, C: partial thickness wound, D: full thickness wound.

Components of each layer

Skin consists of two main layers, the outer epidermis and the underlying dermis. Specialised epidermal structures such as hair follicles and sebaceous and sweat glands lie within the dermis without interrupting the epidermo-dermal junction. Beneath the dermis lies the supporting hypodermis or subcutaneous fatty tissue. It contains nerve fibres and endings, blood vessels supplying the skin, and lymphatics.

Wound depth

Skin wounds can be classified by the layers involved. Superficial wounds involve only the epidermis. Partial thickness wounds involve the dermis. Full thickness wounds reach into the subcutaneous fat or deeper.

Appearance

The dermis is intact if, on examination of a wound, normal skin markings, for example fingerprints, can be identified. A superficial partial thickness injury reveals uniformly pale pink dermis. Injury at a deep dermal level reveals islands of yellow fat penetrating a network of dermis. In full thickness wounds, continuous areas of fat globules are seen without overlying pink dermis. Bleeding from a superficial wound is via numerous punctate bleeding points. In deeper dermal wounds, larger more widely separated sources of bleeding are seen. Full thickness, penetrating wounds may exhibit pulsatile arterial bleeding or slow venous oozing.

At what level does a simple traumatic blister form?

The Epidermis

When damage is superficial, affecting only the epidermis, healing is by regeneration.

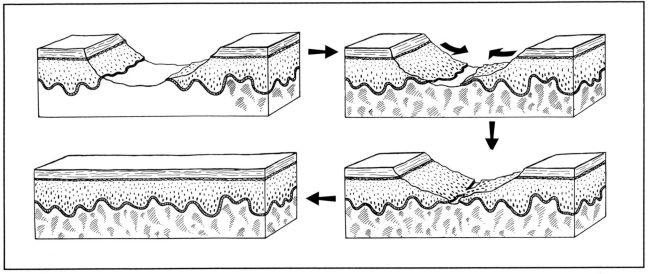

Migration of epithelial cells across wound surface during regeneration.

Physiological replacement

The epidermis has five cellular strata. Cells of the basal cell layer continually divide. Older cells are displaced towards the surface where they are eventually shed. A gradual maturation process transforms the round, nucleated cells of the basal layer into the flattened, keratin rich squames found on the outer surface of the epidermis. These cells are dead.

Squames G

Repair

Repair of damaged epidermis occurs by regeneration, a process similar to physiological epidermal replacement. The cells of the basal layer multiply, then migrate in a leap-frog fashion from undamaged areas to replace damaged cells. The eventual repair has a normal structure and appearance and leaves no visible scar.

Regeneration G

Scar 101

Artificial skin

It is now possible to grow sheets of epidermal cells in the laboratory. Research projects have used small samples of a patient's skin to provide cells for culture. These grow into an epithelial sheet which may be used to resurface the patient's wound. There are still many problems associated with these techniques, eg the time taken to produce a sheet of any size. These projects are the first steps towards artificially produced skin.

Culture

Cultured keratinocytes and grafts. Hancock K and Leigh I. Br Med J 1989; **299**: 1179.

Regeneration of epidermis by cells grown in tissue culture. Eisinger M. J Am Acad Dermatol 1985; **12**: 402-448.

Cultured composite skin grafts for burns. Nonchahal J, Davies D. Br Med J 1990; **301**: 1342.

The Dermis

Damage affecting the dermis heals by granulation tissue formation.

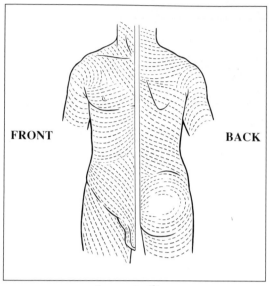

FRONT   BACK

Langer's Lines

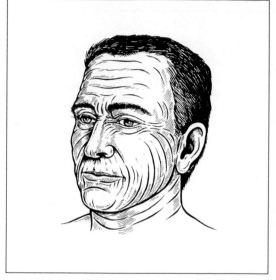

Wrinkle lines redrawn from Kraissl

Components of dermis

The dermis consists of collagen and elastin fibres in a mucopolysaccharide matrix, supplied by a rich capillary network. The dermis supports the epidermis. Dermal elastin supplies the elasticity and collagen provides the tensile strength of the skin. Dermal thickness and hence strength varies in different parts of the body. Compare the feel of the skin of the back with that of the eyelid.

Elastin G
Mucopolysaccharide G
Matrix G
Capillary 87
Collagen G
Strength 93

Dermal repair

Damage to the dermis is repaired by a process called granulation. The proportion of the constituents and the architecture of the repair differ from that of normal dermis. Healed superficial dermal damage may be clinically indistinguishable from normal skin. Deep dermal damage results in the formation of a permanent, visible repair or scar. The tensions across a wound affect the way new collagen is laid down in a healing wound, the strength of the eventual scar and its appearance.

Granulation 99

Collagen G
Scar 101

Siting of surgical incisions

Skin tension was first mapped by Langer in the last century in fresh unpreserved corpses. For the best cosmetic result surgical wounds on the body and limbs should be sited, when practicable, along the relaxed skin tension lines as described by Borges. Facial incisions should follow the natural wrinkle lines as described by Kraissl. Although transverse abdominal skin incisions are preferred for cosmetic reasons, vertical incisions are sometimes required for better access to the abdomen.

Lines

On the Anatomy and physiology of the skin II: skin tension. Langer K. Brit J Plast Surg 1978; **3**: 93-106.

Zur anatomie und physiologie der haut IV. Das quellungvermogen der cutis. Langer R. Shzungsber Math CL Kaiserlich Acad Wiss 1862; **45**: 192.

Relaxed Skin Tension Lines (RSTL) versus other skin lines. Borges A F. Plast Reconstr Surg 1984; **73**: 144-150.

The selection of apppropiriate lines for elective surgical incisions. Kraissl C J. Plast Reconstr Surg 1951; **8**: 1.

The Epidermal Appendages

The epidermal appendages have an important role to play when wounding affects the dermis.

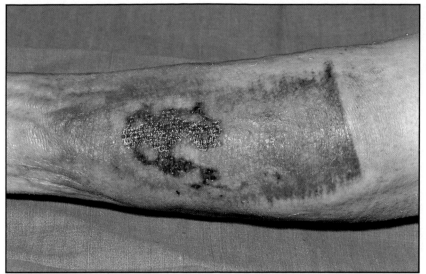

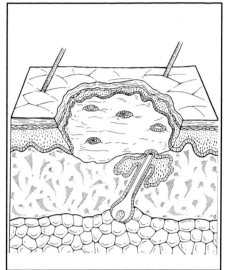

Islands of regenerating epithelium spreading to cover the wound.

Epidermo-dermal junction

The junction of the epidermis and dermis forms a series of waves called rete ridges or pegs. Epidermal appendages, such as hair follicles and sweat glands, are lined by epidermal cells and dip down into the dermis without interrupting the epidermo-dermal junction.

Partial thickness repair

Partial thickness damage to skin may leave viable epidermal cells in the base of the ridges or dermal part of the appendages. These form islands of epidermal cells within a sea of dermis. Repair of the epidermis occurs by migration and multiplication of cells from these islands until they form a continuous sheet, healing the wound. Infection of a superficial wound can destroy remaining epidermal elements, reducing the wound's ability to re-epithelialise.

Loss of epidermal appendages

If the hair follicles, sebaceous glands or sweat glands in an area are completely destroyed by injury or infection, they cannot regenerate. Resulting scar tissue tends to crack and fissure as it lacks normal lubricating sebum. It will also be hairless. This is particularly significant in areas such as the scalp, where a bald patch is a cosmetic problem. The scalp is frequently involved when a toddler is scalded. Even if the burn is superficial, hair loss may result if the wound subsequently becomes infected.

Epidermis 83
Dermis 84

Repair 100

Infection 105

Nerves of the Skin

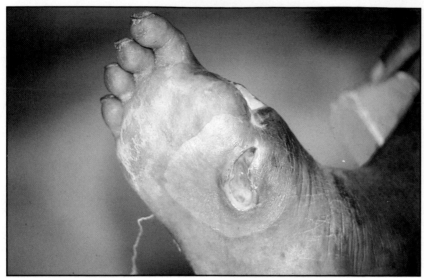

Ulceration and toe loss in a patient with leprosy

Sensory function

The skin is a sensory organ, collecting information via an extensive neuronal network and nerve-endings. These provide information on pressure, vibration, pain and temperature. External hazards are detected and avoiding action can be taken to minimise damage. Injury is associated with the release of chemical mediators which stimulate pain nerve endings of A (delta) fibres and C fibres entering the spinal cord through the dorsal root.

Nerve-endings

Mediators 94 G

Loss of sensory function

Risk of injury is greatly increased by lack of sensation. Sensory loss may result from acute division of a peripheral sensory nerve or chronic nerve damage. Further injury to the area supplied may then occur as no warning of the proximity of a hazard can be transmitted.

Important neuropathies

Diabetic neuropathy significantly decreases sensation in the lower limbs. The fast-conduction nerve fibres (eg A (alpha) proprioception and A (delta) pain) are affected by vascular damage, vibration sense being lost first. The patient receives no warning of injury or onset of infection in a minor wound. As diabetes also causes abnormalities in the healing processes and vascular supply, such wounds may result in persistent ulceration. Leprosy causes gradual destruction of nerves by bacterial invasion and the immunological response to this. Anaesthetic extremities become liable to injury with resultant marked deformity.

Diabetic 128

Neuropathy 86
Proprioception G

Leprosy G

Can you think of any other conditions where impaired sensation contributes to tissue damage?

Morphology of cutaneous receptors. Iggo A and Andres K H. Ann Rev Neuro Surg 1982; **5**: 1.

Management of the insensitive limb. Brand P W. Phys Ther 1979; **59**: 8-12.

Vascular Supply

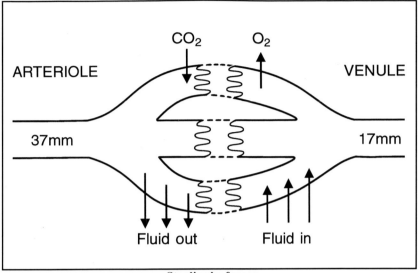

ARTERIOLE CO_2 O_2 VENULE

37mm   17mm

Fluid out   Fluid in

Starling's forces

Role of the blood supply

Skin possesses an extensive network of dermal capillaries which are fed by arterioles. They drain into venules in the subdermal tissues. All tissues require oxygen, nutrients and a way of eliminating carbon dioxide and waste products. This exchange between the bloodstream and interstitial fluid occurs across the capillary wall. The vascular system is lined by endothelial cells. These have many properties and are involved in the initiation of healing and clotting.

Starling's forces

The normal capillary is supplied with blood at a pressure of 37mm Hg. Blood in the venule is at 17mm Hg. The capillary is subjected to an osmotic pressure gradient as well as hydrostatic pressures (Starling's forces). Tissue fluid tends to form at the arterial end of a skin capillary and is reabsorbed at the venous end.

Regional differences

Capillary density and blood supply to skin vary in different regions of the body. Facial and scalp injuries bleed profusely because of the rich blood supply. The well vascularised tissue heals rapidly, and ischaemic complications are rare. In contrast, lower leg wounds have a more meagre blood supply, especially in older patients as blood supply to the skin decreases with age. Ischaemia may result in necrosis or delayed healing.

Skin flaps

Skin flaps raised on the face can be orientated in any direction. Their base to length ratio may be greater than the 1:1 quoted for skin in general, without suffering ischaemic complications. In the leg, flaps of skin raised on inferiorly orientated bases will have greatly reduced blood supply and decreased survival. It is important to remember this when treating the relatively common superficial leg injuries seen in casualty.

Clotting 92

Fluid 141

Age 107
Necrosis 140 G

Flap G

Ischaemia G

87

Section 3
Stage: The Healing Processes

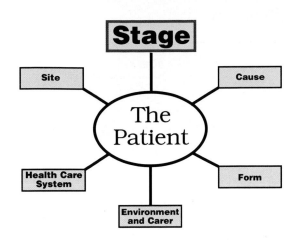

The Wound Organiser

The previous section considered the effects of damage to skin. Now use the second aspect of the Organiser to look at how skin heals and what affects the rate of healing.

Consult the Guide to Section 3 on page 90. If you are familiar with the stages of healing move on to another section

Stages of Healing Process

Stage	Process	Clinical Effects
Immediate Haemostasis	Vasoconstriction. Activation of endothelial cells, platelets, and clotting cascade.	Haemorrhage controlled or reduced. Clot forms in wound.
Inflammation Mediator release	Cell stimulation/inhibition.	Inflammatory process initiated. Pain.
Vasodilation	Increased blood flow.	Skin becomes red, hot.
Increased capillary permeability	Protein, cells and fluid leak from capillaries.	Swelling. Exudate production.
Chemotaxis	Mediators attract phagocytes (neutrophils first, then macrophages).	Contribute to exudate and swelling.
Phagocytosis	Neutrophils and macrophages remove debris and bacteria.	Crust, pus or sloughing.
Initiation of repair	Macrophages produce growth factor.	No clinical effects visible.
Proliferation Granulation:		Red, vascular tissue appears in wound.
• angiogenesis	Endothelial budding of marginal capillaries.	
• collagen production	Fibroblasts migrate to the scene and secrete collagen.	
Epithelialisation	Epithelial cell multiplication and migration over surface.	Smooth marginal zone or islands of epithelium seen in wound.
Contraction	Possibly due to specialised fibroblast action.	Size of defect reduced.
Maturation Collagen remodelling	Type III collagen converted to Type I, increasing strength.	Scar flattens and softens.
Capillary regression	Reduction in number of vessels, reducing blood flow.	Scar pales, itching subsides.

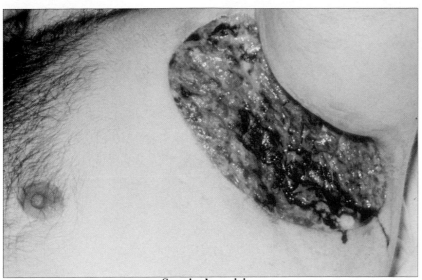

Surgical excision

How to control bleeding

A firm compression bandage with elevation of the injured part controls bleeding from most wounds. A tourniquet should not normally be used. When a larger vessel is partially divided, vasoconstriction and clotting may not control the defect and bleeding continues. In these cases, surgical exploration and ligation or repair of the vessel will be required before bleeding can be controlled. Vascular surgery may also be required to restore circulation to a devascularised part when a large vessel is divided.

If bleeding continues.

If, in spite of compression bandaging and surgical intervention, bleeding continues, the integrity of the clotting process should be investigated. Tests should be performed to identify any deficiency in the clotting process and appropriate replacement therapy should be instituted.

Haematoma

A collection of blood in a wound is called a haematoma. It may be partially clotted. Haematoma predisposes to infection and delays healing.

Clotting

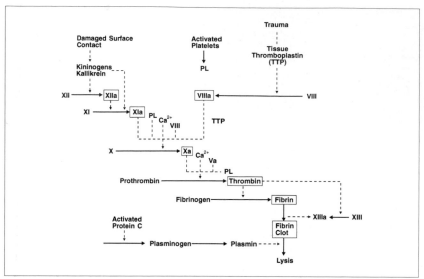

The clotting cascade

Post wounding

Tissue damage triggers a number of processes and activates various cells and cellular elements. It leads to the release of a large number of chemical mediators, and intercell messenger substances, called cytokines. These molecules may be either growth or inhibitory factors and may initiate a complex interrelated series of events, leading to haemostasis and healing.

The platelet plug

When blood vessels are damaged, platelets, activated by exposed collagen in vessel walls, become sticky and adhere to the wall and each other. Platelets aggregate by the action of thromboxane A_2, a prostaglandin synthesised by activated platelets. They thus form a temporary plug at the site of vessel injury. Prostacyclin produced by endothelial cells prevents platelet adhesion on an undamaged endothelial surface. Platelets also release serotonin and other vasoconstrictors in response to injury. This helps to limit immediate blood loss by constricting the severed vessels.

Clotting cascade

Injury to the vascular endothelium also initiates the clotting cascade. Damaged vessel wall, platelets and coagulation factors are the three components that interact in clot formation. The mechanisms of the clotting process are illustrated above. The end product of each reaction in the cascade activates the next. Calcium ions and phospholipids are necessary at many stages for clotting reactions to occur. These reactions produce thrombin, which forms the clot by converting fibrinogen to fibrin. Fibrin then forms a mesh, which acts as a framework and traps cellular elements of the blood. The fibrin mesh also helps to stabilise the platelet plug.

Control of clotting

Normally the clotting cascade is precisely regulated. Once a clot has formed in response to injury and has served its purpose it is lysed by plasmin, a serine protease acting on fibrin. Plasmin is formed by activation of plasminogen present in plasma.

The degradation products of fibrin and other mediators produced in response to injury exert many in vitro effects. These include increased collagen synthesis by fibroblasts, chemotaxis of macrophages, and enhanced vessel permeability. The exact role of some of these in the control of healing is still to be established.

The Phases of Healing

Healing comprises three overlapping phases: inflammation, proliferation and maturation.

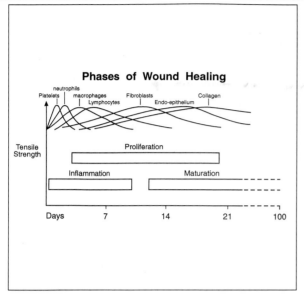

Phases of Wound Healing

Tensile Strength

Proliferation

Inflammation   Maturation

Days   7   14   21   100

Relationship of levels of wound constituents to time and phases of healing.

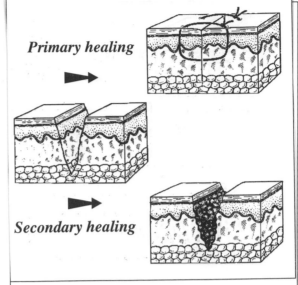

Primary healing

Secondary healing

Primary and secondary healing

Control of healing

 Healing has three phases, which overlap:

- inflammation,
- proliferation,
- maturation.

Healing is complete when the skin surface has reformed and the skin has regained most of its tensile strength.

Role of mediators

 Healing consists of a series of processes, the extent and timing of which are controlled by a multiplicity of mediators. The roles of those mediators which have been identified are under investigation and new mediators are still being isolated. It is clear that some mediators may be both inhibitory and stimulatory and that there is duplication of roles. This redundancy means that a defect in one system of control may impede healing but seldom blocks it.

Primary and secondary healing

 A clean cut which is closed by suturing requires the formation of only a small amount of new tissue. This is called primary healing. In a traumatic wound where tissue is lost, the defect must be filled with new tissue and then covered by epithelium. This is secondary healing. Primary healing is achieved much more rapidly, within a matter of days. Secondary healing can take weeks or months, depending on the site and size of the defect.

Inflammation 94 G
Proliferation 98 G
Maturation 101 G

Strength 99

Mediators 94

Primary 111, 136

Secondary 111,

 Epidermal cytokines and their roles in cutaneous wound healing. McKay I A and Leigh I M. J Dermatol 1991; **124**: 513-518.

Inflammation

The first response to tissue damage is inflammation: it has five cardinal signs.

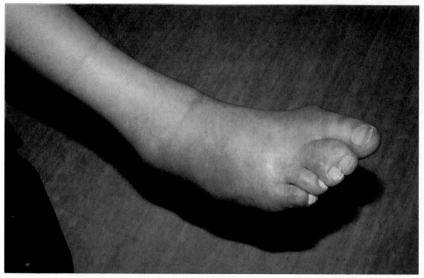

In wound healing studies, the challenge of the nineties will be to ascertain which cytokine activities are important.

An inflamed foot showing some of the cardinal signs of inflammation.

Initiation

Inflammation is the body's initial response to injury. It activates protective mechanisms and prepares the tissues for the following phases. Inflammation is mediated by release of a number of chemical substances (mediators), e.g. leukotrienes, complement fragments such as C5a, platelet activating factor (PAF), fibrin degradation products (FDP) serotonin and histamine. The release of mediators in the wound results in vasodilation, increased capillary permeability, and stimulation of pain fibres.

Leukotrienes G
Complement G
Fibrin degradation products 92
Histamine G
Mediators 95

Cardinal signs

There are five cardinal signs of inflammation:

- heat,
- redness,
- pain,
- swelling
- loss of function.

Signs 105

In a clean cut closed by suturing, these signs are usually minimal and transitory. In traumatic wounds with diffuse damage, the inflammatory response is more prominent and lasts longer. Inflammation is greatly intensified and prolonged by infection. An infected red, hot, and oedematous area of skin is called cellulitis. Debility in the elderly, diabetes mellitus, and steroids all depress the inflammatory response. This may make clinical detection of an early wound infection more difficult.

Suturing 162

Infection 105
Oedematous G
Cellulitis G
Elderly 107
Diabetes 128 G
Steroids 130 G

What is the triple response? Make a linear scratch on your arm and note what changes occur in the skin.

Inflammatory Exudate

Wound inflammation leads to production of inflammatory exudate, an important part of the wound's defence system.

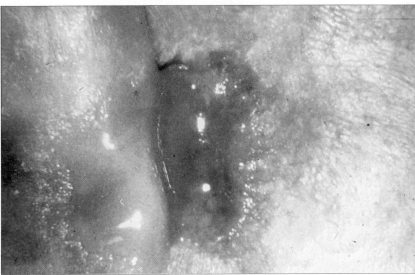

Exudate trapped under an occlusive dressing.

Exudate formation

Increase in permeability of small vessels within a wound allows leakage of a protein rich fluid. Mediators, released during inflammation, attract a variety of cells into the area by chemotaxis. As a result, an inflammatory exudate is formed on the wound surface. It contains phagocytic cells and a mixture of proteins, including antibodies and polypeptides of the complement system. The volume of exudate is proportional to the surface area of the wound. It will increase where the tissues are oedematous or the inflammation intense.

Exudate forms an important part of the wound's defence system. It acts as a medium for phagocytic cells and enzymes. Soon after injury, neutrophils are attracted to the area. After about 72 hours, monocyte derived macrophages become the dominant cell type, clearing dead cells and bacteria. Macrophages serve as a trigger for other cells to appear in the wound by releasing factors such as leukotrienes.

Properties of exudate

A wound produces exudate until epithelialisation is complete. Seen as a yellow stain on any dressing, it is a normal part of the healing process. Exudate is kept in contact with the wound by occlusive dressings. Researchers have recently proposed that growth promoting substances in exudate lead to enhanced healing in chronic wounds.

Exudate G 166

Neutrophil G

Epithelialisation G

Occlusive 165 G

Autolysis

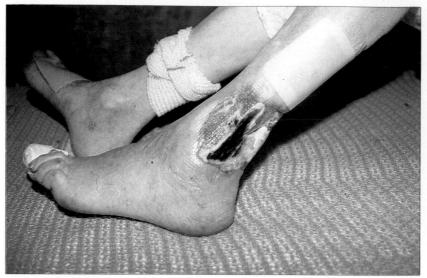

Granulating leg ulcer with an area of necrotic material.

What is autolysis?

Autolysis is natural degradation of devitalised tissue. Enzymes, eg acid hydrolases, normally confined to lysosomes, are released at cell death. They digest cell contents and produce tissue necrosis. Polymorph neutrophils and, later, macrophages are attracted to damaged and necrotic tissue. They release further enzymes, which help digest debris. A layer of separation eventually develops between viable tissue and the overlying necrotic material or scab.

Autolysis G

Lysosomes G
Necrosis 140
Polymorph G

Scab G

Natural debridement in a burn

The intense heat of a burn denatures protein, destroys enzymes and prevents the initial enzymatic activity of necrosis. Therefore natural debridement depends on phagocytic activity of neutrophils and macrophages. Bacteria may also degrade some debris.

Debridement 119 G

Moist environment

Autolysis, being an active process involving enzymes and cells, requires a moist environment. Measures which prevent drying out promote autolysis. Modern synthetic dressings, eg hydrocolloids, hydrogels and films, provide a moist wound environment and promote sloughing of necrotic tissue by autolysis. However, tissue desiccation retards microbial overgrowth and this is occasionally utilised, eg the mummified diabetic toe which is kept dry until it separates.

Moist environment 165

Hydrocolloid G
Hydrogel G

Gangrene

Gangrene is a time-honoured synonym for tissue necrosis. Dry gangrene is uninfected necrotic tissue. Wet gangrene implies superadded infection. Gas gangrene is a term used to denote infection of necrotic tissue with anaerobic gas-producing bacteria from the genus Clostridia.

Gangrene G
Gas gangrene 173

Immunology

Body's defences

The immune system forms the body's natural defences. All elements of the immune system influence the healing process. Both aspects of the immune system (antibody and cell mediated) are necessary to mount an adequate defence against invasion by bacteria. The principal cells in the immune response are lymphocytes, monocytes and macrophages. Other cell types such as keratinocytes, endothelial cells and fibroblasts play a part in initiation and regulation of the responses. Phagocytes are responsible for non-specific defence. Specific responses are provided by antibody production and T-cell mediated immunity.

Decreased immunity

Patients with decreased immunity may show poor healing. Increasingly, patients with AIDS, patients successfully treated for conditions such as leukaemia, or those treated with irradiation or immunosuppressive drugs will highlight the importance of the immune system in healing. Decreased immunity may also play a part in the healing problems experienced by patients suffering from major burns or pressure sores.

Immune aspects of wound repairs. Bartul A. Clin Plast Surg 1990; **17**(3): 433.

Defence   105
Immune
system G
Antibody   G

Lymphocyte G
Keratinocyte G
Phagocytes 96 G

Decreased
immunity   130

Burns 119
Pressure sores
125 G

97

Proliferation

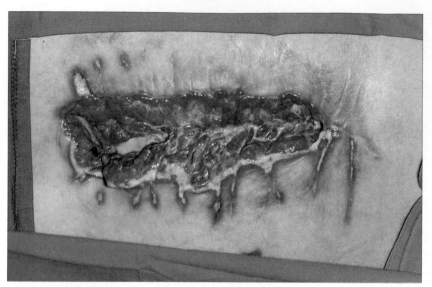

Granulation tissue forming after breakdown of a surgical wound.

Processes in proliferation

A phase of new tissue proliferation follows the initial inflammatory response. This reparative phase involves three processes.

- **Granulation** leads to the formation of a network of new blood vessels (angiogenesis) in a collagen rich matrix. Chemotaxis attracts mesenchymal cells to the wound. These differentiate into fibroblasts which synthesise the collagen.
- **Contraction** minimises the size of the wound.
- **Epithelialisation** resurfaces the wound by regenerating epithelium.

What you see

Granulation tissue can be seen forming a reddish, velvety carpet in the base of healing ulcers. Contraction is a gradual process and is therefore not often appreciated in the clinical setting. However, it may significantly decrease the area to be covered by epithelium. In a healing ulcer, a marginal zone of smooth tissue may be identified. This is the advancing epithelium. The balance between granulation and contraction depends on site and tissue laxity. For example, varicose ulcers exist in a fibrous bed and cannot undergo contraction. A yellow fibrinous membrane is often seen in healthy granulating wounds and should not be confused with infection.

Contraction

Wound contraction may be a function of differentiated wound fibroblasts which contain actin and myosin fibrils. These are present in large numbers in contracting wounds. Contraction is inhibited by full thickness skin grafts though the mechanism is not yet clear. Since contraction may have either beneficial or undesirable clinical effects, further research in this area is essential. Such contraction should be differentiated from scar contracture seen in the final phase of healing.

Presence of modified fibroblasts in granulation tissue and their possible role in wound contraction. Gabbiani G, Ryan G B and Mayno G. Experientia 1971; **27**: 549-550.

Inhibition of myofibroblasts by skin grafts. Rudolph R. Plast Reconstr Surg 1979; **63**: 473-480.

Granulation 99
Angiogenesis G

Contraction G

Epithelialisation 100

Granulation tissue G

Fibrous bed 122

Fibroblasts G

Skin graft G

Contracture G 101

Granulation Tissue

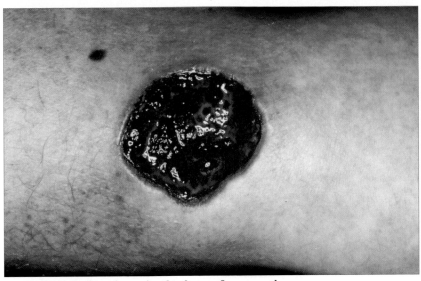

Granulation tissue in the base of a wound.

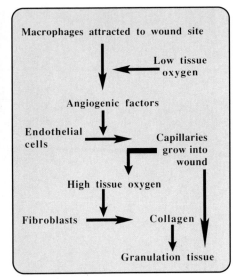

Macrophages attracted to wound site

Low tissue oxygen

Angiogenic factors

Endothelial cells → Capillaries grow into wound

High tissue oxygen

Fibroblasts → Collagen

Granulation tissue

Cells involved in granulation

 Granulation tissue formation begins approximately five days after injury. Macrophages, fibroblasts and blood vessels enter the wound space together and are interdependent. The macrophages are attracted to the wound and secrete a number of growth factors and chemotactic factors in response to low tissue oxygen tension. Examples of growth factors are platelet-derived growth factor, fibroblast growth factor and transitional growth factor - beta. The fibroblasts respond to these growth and chemotactic factors in the wound by multiplication, migration and matrix deposition. Endothelial cells of blood vessels also respond by forming new capillaries which grow into the wound (angiogenesis). The collagen rich matrix secreted by the fibroblasts provides a substrate for macrophages, fibroblasts and new blood vessels. The vessels, in turn, provide nutrients and oxygen for continued growth.

Collagen

Vitamin C acts as a co-enzyme for the hydroxylation of proline in collagen to hydroxyproline. Hydroxyproline allows for cross linkages of collagen fibres. Collagen produced in the absence of vitamin C (in scurvy) cannot form into fibres by cross linkages and is easily degraded. A scar formed in the absence of vitamin C is therefore weaker.

Interactive dressings

There is still much to discover about how wound repair is initiated, controlled and terminated. Cells, matrix and mediators interact, inducing a chain reaction. Researchers have looked into how dressings affect these reactions. Occlusion, particularly with certain hydrocolloids, promotes angiogenesis. Hydrocolloids are possibly chemotactic for macrophages. Studies of hydrocolloid dressings indicate that they differ in their fibrinolytic activity. This may alter their effect on the wound. These findings open the way to the development of dressings which are truly interactive with the healing wound.

Oxygen tension 103

Scurvy G
Scar 101

Epithelialisation

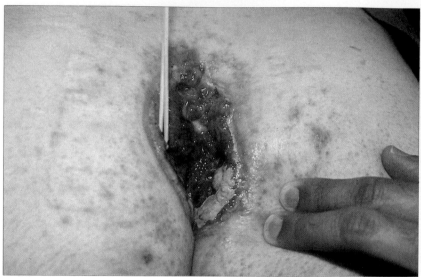

Epithelialisation of a full thickness wound healing by granulation

Capillary ingrowth

High tissue oxygen

Collagen formation

Epithelial cells

Granulation tissue

Supports

Epithelialisation

Margin of new epithelium forming after pilonidal sinus excision.

Resurfacing

Epithelialisation resurfaces the wound. In a full thickness wound, regeneration occurs from epithelial cells in the wound margins. In a partial thickness wound, remnants of partially ablated hair follicles will also contribute to re-epithelialisation. Epithelial cells multiply and migrate to cover the wound. The measurable size of the wound decreases until a continuous sheet is formed. Further migration is halted by contact inhibition, a complex process of interrelated mechanisms. Initially, attachment of the new surface to underlying tissue is fragile and easily disrupted.

Regeneration 83

Hair follicles 85

Contact inhibition G

Influences on epithelialisation

Research shows that the rate of epithelialisation may be enhanced by a moist local environment maintained, for instance, by occlusive dressings. Other factors which may affect epithelialisation are temperature and pH. Epithelisation is delayed by foreign material, desiccation and infection. Frequent dressing changes may disrupt the delicate new epithelium.

Moist environment 165

Control of epithelialisation

In uninjured skin, the basal keratinocytes are in contact with glycoproteins, such as laminin, which inhibit migration. These glycoproteins allow the epithelial cells to attach to underlying connective tissue. Injury brings the keratinocytes into contact with other molecules, eg collagen or fibronectin, which appear to promote locomotion. Migrating epithelial cells move over a provisional matrix of fibrin and fibronectin. A new basal membrane then forms from the wound margins inward, the provisional matrix dissipating.

Laminin G
Connective tissue G

Provisional matrix

Fibronectin G

Fibronectin and fibrin provide a provisional matrix for epidermal cell migration during wound epithelisation. Clark R A F. J Invest Derm 1982; **79**: 264-269.

Epidermal wound healing. Maibach H I and Rovee D T. Chicago: Yearbook Medical Publishers, 1972.

Connective-tissue proteins. In: Biochemistry. Stryer L. New York: W H Freeman, 1988.

100

Maturation

Maturation, the third phase of healing, follows proliferation. The repair is reorganised.

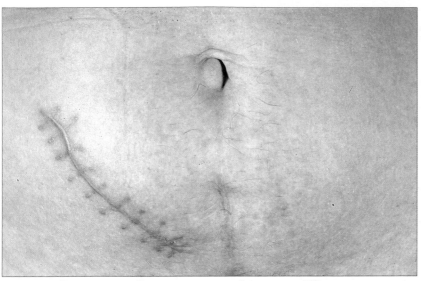
Recent appendicectomy scar and mature midline scar.

Remodelling

In maturation the Type III collagen, laid down during proliferation, is converted to Type I and undergoes extensive reorganisation. Once the collagen bed is established, the total amount remains stable but a dynamic balance exists between destruction and synthesis. As remodelling progresses, cellular activity reduces, and the number of blood vessels in the repair decreases.

The visible scar

Initially the uncomplicated linear scar has an acceptable flat appearance. Then the scar becomes red, firm, and raised. In time, maturation causes the scar to fade, soften, and become flatter. It may stretch.

The hypertrophic scar

In some patients, the proliferative phase of healing may be prolonged. Large amounts of collagen are laid down and the normal features of the scar are accentuated. The scar is very red, indurated and raised. This scar is described as hypertrophic and it takes longer to mature, possibly years. Deep dermal burn scars in children may result in hypertrophic scars and will take up to two years to soften. Elasticated garments, which apply pressure to the scar, are used to hasten maturation in the treatment of hypertrophic scars.

Contracture

During maturation, shortening or contracture of the scar may occur because of reorganisation of collagen as a reaction to stretching and extension. This should not be confused with contraction of the wound. Contracture, combined with the scar's lack of elasticity, can cause clinical problems of tightness or limitation of joint mobility. In children growth and development may be affected. For example diffuse anterior chest scarring in a young girl may require surgical release and grafting to allow the breasts to develop normally.

The fundamentals of wound management. Hunt T K and Dumphy J E (eds). New York: Appleton, Century, Crofts, 1979.

The biosynthesis of collagen and its disorders. Prockop D J, Kivirikko K I, Tuderman L and Guzman N A. N Eng J Med 1979; **301**: 13-23, 77-85.

Collagen 99

Scar 84

Collagen

Hypertrophic G

Contracture G

Contraction 98

Scarring 119

101

The Healed Wound

Healing continues long after the wound is resurfaced.

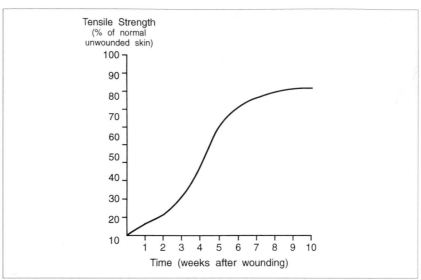

Graph showing relationship between tensile strength and time after wounding

When is a wound healed?

Normally the wound is considered healed when it has been resurfaced with epithelium. It appears pink, smooth and dry. The surface layer has been reconstituted and fluid exudate ceases. However, the process of healing continues for some time after this. The surface epithelium matures by differentiation into a stratified structure. Remodelling of collagen continues and the number of capillaries gradually decreases.

Scar strength

Where full thickness dermal damage has occurred, the wound is initially weak though its strength gradually increases with remodelling. A scar never completely regains the tensile strength of surrounding undamaged skin.

Keloids

Keloid scars form when control of proliferation and maturation is abnormal. The scar is hard, raised and possibly painful or pruritic. It may extend into surrounding tissue, not originally traumatised. Excision of keloid scars is not usually recommended, because there is a high incidence of recurrence and the resulting keloid may be worse than the original. Intra-lesional injection of steroids is used in the treatment of keloids as they inhibit fibroblast activity. Exceptionally, excision and suture or excision and graft of keloid accompanied by low dose radiotherapy given immediately before or after the operation may be employed.

Court cases

Scarring from road traffic accidents or assaults may be the subject of police investigation, legal action or compensation hearings. In these situations the number of stitches involved is often used in evidence. Court proceedings can cause anxiety and confused motivation during rehabilitation. It may take several years for such legal proceedings to be completed and this may prolong rehabilitation.

Resurfaced   100

Exudate 95

Remodelling 101

Strength 84

Keloid G

Can collagen metabolism be controlled? Theoretical considerations. Cohen I K. J Trauma 1985; **25**: 410-412.

Keloids: a review. Murray J C, Pollock S V and Pinnell S R. Clin J Am Acad Dermatol 1981; **4**(4): 461-470.

Rate of Healing

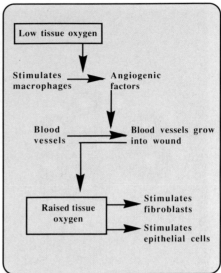

Optimal healing conditions

For optimal healing, there must be an adequate supply of nutrients and energy, with effective removal of waste products. The wound should be mechanically stable, moist, warm and free from contaminants, infection and dead tissue.

Factors affecting healing

Healing is affected by a myriad of different factors. These may be local factors, relating to the type of wound, its site, the blood supply to the area or the presence of haematoma. General factors reflecting the condition of the patient are also important. One or more adverse factors are usually present when delayed healing or failure to heal occurs.

Oxygen levels

The oxygen level in tissue has been shown to affect the rate of healing. A low tissue oxygen level at the advancing edge of proliferation creates an oxygen gradient which stimulates macrophages to produce angiogenic factors. These attract blood vessels into the wound which raises oxygen tension. This provides the energy for fibroblasts to lay down collagen and for epithelialisation.

Smoking has been shown to reduce oxygen tension in the blood and subcutaneous tissue of wounds. The level of hypoxia produced by smoking is associated with poor healing. This hypoxia lasts for some time after each cigarette smoked. It is thought to be due to a nicotine-induced vasoconstriction. Smokers have an increased risk of skin flap necrosis and peripheral ulcers.

Regulation of wound healing angiogenesis - effect of oxygen gradients and inspired oxygen concentration. Knighton D, Silver I A and Hunt T K. Surgery 1981; **90**: 262.

Cigarette smoking decreases tissue oxygen. Jensen J A, Goodson W H, Hopf H W and Hunt T K. Arch Surg 1991; **126**: 1131-1134.

Haematoma 91

Oxygen level 99

Smoking Hypoxia G

Micro-organisms

Wounds allow micro-organisms to gain entry to deep tissues.

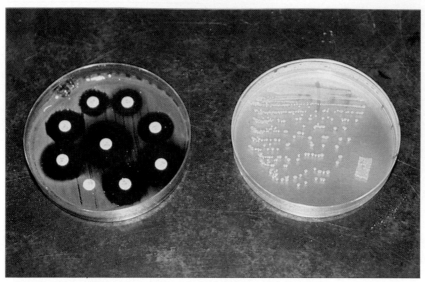

Bacterial colonies growing on culture plates.

Bacteria and the wound

Diagnosis of infection

Commensals and pathogens

 The presence of bacteria on the surface of a wound but not invading the underlying tissue is termed colonisation. A skin infection is caused by the invasion of organisms into viable tissue causing clinical signs. Bacterial species vary in their ability to invade living tissue and in the initial number required to cause infection. Some bacteria produce poisons, called toxins, which can have local or systemic effects on the host.

When an infection is suspected on clinical grounds, a surface swab is used to sample the wound's bacteria. Culture and identification of these bacteria provides useful information as to the likely invasive organisms. A more reliable, but invasive, method of accurately diagnosing infection is tissue biopsy and culture. When systemic infection is suspected clinically, it may be confirmed by growing organisms from blood samples.

Skin wounds are commonly colonised by bacteria, eg non-pathogenic streptococci, staphylococci and pseudomonas. These and other bacteria may produce a wound infection. Wound infections may also be caused by fungi and these infections tend to be commoner in certain geographic regions. In the UK, fungal infections are more commonly associated with immunocompromised patients.

Colonisation G

Signs 105

Toxins 161 G

104

Infection

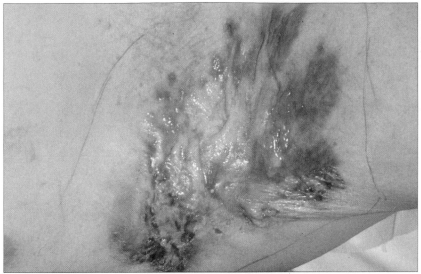

Infection of axillary skin

When infection occurs

 The destruction of an intact skin layer provides a portal of entry for micro-organisms. The first line of defence against a wound infection is the immune system, which recognises and destroys invading organisms. Infection occurs only when this destructive capacity is overwhelmed and micro-organisms invade living tissue. The presence of necrotic tissue, foreign bodies or haematoma increases the wound's susceptibility to infection, as do a number of systemic conditions, eg diabetes.

Intact skin 81
Defence 97

Foreign bodies 114
Haematoma 91
Diabetes 128

Consequences of infection

A wound infection may cause

- intense inflammation of the wound,
- pus,
- a rise in the white blood cell count (WBC),
- pyrexia.

Inflammation 94
Pus G

Pyrexia G

Large burns cause some of these effects, such as pyrexia or an altered white blood count. The subsequent onset of infection of the burn may therefore be masked. Infection of a wound delays healing and causes additional tissue damage. This may precipitate wound dehiscence. Bacteria may spread into the bloodstream causing bacteraemia or septicaemia with sometimes fatal results. After a wound complication, scarring is likely to be less cosmetically acceptable.

Dehiscence G
Bacteraemia G
Septicaemia G
Complication 111
Wound complication G

Nutritional Status

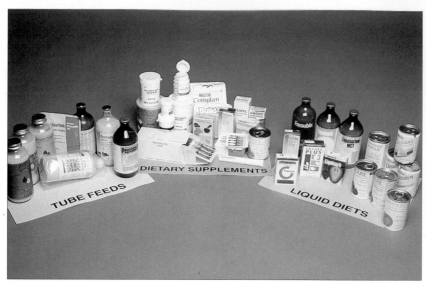

Many different ways exist to improve a patient's nutrition.

Supply of nutrients

Healing requires adequate supplies of protein and calories in addition to certain vitamins and trace elements, eg vitamin C, zinc. Problems occur if supplies are inadequate due to poor intake (starvation or malnutrition), abnormal absorption (gastrointestinal tract disease or surgery), or greatly increased demands (extensive burns).

Vitamin C 99

Dietary imbalance

Dietary deficiencies may be obvious or subtle and clinically silent. Patients with chronic wounds, such as pressure sores, may have increased metabolic demands and usually need nutritional supplements and a raised calorie intake. Calorie requirements are also greatly increased in patients with extensive burns or trauma, where the basal metabolic rate is raised and a catabolic state exists. Obesity may also give rise to problems with wound healing. It increases the wound complication rate following surgery, affects general fitness and mobility and may exacerbate conditions such as venous hypertension.

Pressure sores 132

Metabolic rate G
Catabolic G
Complication 113
Venous hypertension G

Assessing dietary status

Assessment of dietary status requires a number of different measurements. These include physical measurements, such as height, weight and triceps skin-fold thickness and biochemical estimations, such as serum albumin and transferrin levels. Some or all of these measures may be appropriate, depending on the patient and the condition.

Triceps G
Albumin G
Transferrin G

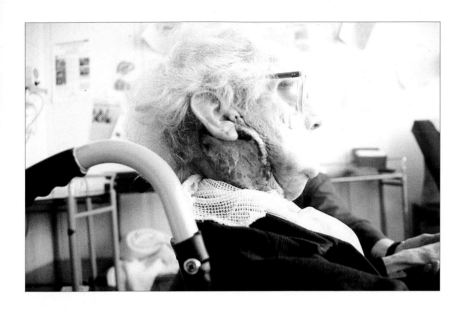

The effect of age

Age has a profound effect on healing. Children have a vigorous healing reaction. They heal rapidly but are prone to hypertrophic scar formation. Aging decreases the inflammatory response. In addition collagen metabolism is reduced, angiogenesis is delayed and epithelialisation slowed.

In spite of slower healing, wounds in the elderly generally heal satisfactorily, and often with a good cosmetic result. Even so, it is important to check for correctable adverse factors and to maintain wound support for longer than in the younger patient. The effects of aging are frequently compounded by concurrent malnutrition, vascular insufficiency or systemic disease. Wound dehiscence after abdominal surgery is up to three times more likely in persons over 60 years.

Foetal wound healing

In the last few years research has been carried out into foetal wound healing. It has shown that, in animals, healing of full thickness wounds may occur without leaving a scar and that this depends on the stage of intrauterine development. This has exciting possibilities for future treatment of congenital conditions such as cleft lip. It may also increase our understanding of the differences between development and repair.

Hypertrophic scar 101

Aging

Adverse factors 103

Support 136

Foetal

Comparison of foetal, newborn and adult wound healing by histological, enzyme-histochemical and hydroxide proline determinations. Adzick N S, Harrison M R, Glick P L et al. J Pediatr Surg 1985; **20**(4): 315-319.

The anatomy and pathogenesis of wrinkles. Kligman A M, Zheng P and Lavker R M. Br J Dermatol 1985; **113**: 37-42.

Section 4
Cause: Types of Wound and Ulcer

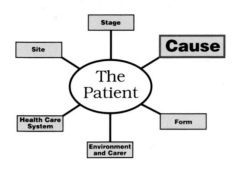

The Wound Organiser

This section deals with the third aspect of the Organiser, the causes of wounds and ulcers. The cause influences skin healing, examined in Section 3, and wound appearance, described in Section 5.

If you have already studied the causes of wounds and ulcers, move on to another section

Aetiology: Acute or Chronic

In this page you will discover why some wounds are called ulcers.

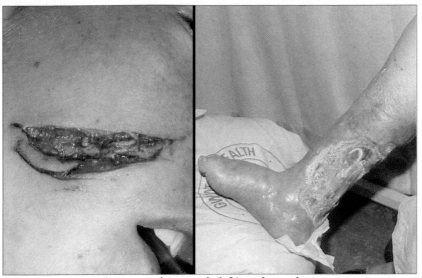

A traumatic wound (left) and an ulcer.

"Healing is a matter of time, but it is sometimes also a matter of opportunity." Hippocrates

Wounds and ulcers

 A wound is a breach in the skin surface which initiates a process of repair. Perhaps the commonest example is a simple cut from a sharp object. An established area of discontinuity that is slow to heal is known as an ulcer or a sore.

Healing time and chronicity

Tissue damage initiates a series of processes which lead, through replacement of damaged tissue, to healing. Where tissue loss is minor, wound edges can be apposed, minimising the necessary repair. This is healing by primary intention. If the area of tissue loss or damage is extensive, the defect fills with granulation tissue, contraction occurs and eventually the wound re-epithelialises. This is healing by secondary intention and requires considerable time.

Healing may be impaired by the presence of adverse conditions. Wounds may be slow to heal or fail to heal, becoming established or "chronic".

Consequences of wounds

 Although acute wounds may have a dramatic effect on the patient's life, they are expected to heal within a predictable time, hopefully without sequelae. However, they may have major long term consequences. For example, a facial laceration heals rapidly but may lead to permanent disfigurement. Chronic wounds are a long term problem and can have a marked influence on the patient's activities, self-image and financial circumstances.

 If a fit young climber sustains a large area of full thickness skin loss that takes months to heal, is this a wound or an ulcer?

Acute Wounds

Knowledge of cause can help you manage wounds more effectively and should alert you when the history does not fit the appearance.

It is but the work of a moment.

How did it happen?

 The skin may be damaged in many ways. It may be cut, torn, burst or crushed by external forces which disrupt cell membranes. It may be rendered non-viable by other forms of physical insult, eg by heat which denatures proteins, or by sub-zero cold leading to intracellular crystal formation. Interruption of the blood supply, chemical attack or the passage of large amounts of electricity can also kill cells.

Cut 113
Crushed 115

Importance of the history

 Knowledge of the aetiology of a wound allows some predictions to be made regarding its physical state and likely consequences. A careful history is an important part of assessing a wound. The nature of the injuring force, eg the temperature of scalding liquid causing a burn or the shape of a penetrating agent, can be a useful predictor of the amount of damage sustained. Similarly, knowledge of how long ago the injury occurred may be important for predicting the likely onset of complications.

Burn 117
Penetrating 114

A history that is not in accordance with the nature of the wound seen on examination should raise questions. The patient may not wish to reveal the true circumstances of the injury for a number of reasons. He or she may be embarrassed, the activity involved may have been illegal or there may be social reasons for concealment. When the patient is a child, the possibility of non-accidental injury must be considered.

Non-accidental injury G

Non-accidental injuries. Speight N. Br Med J 1989; 298: 879.

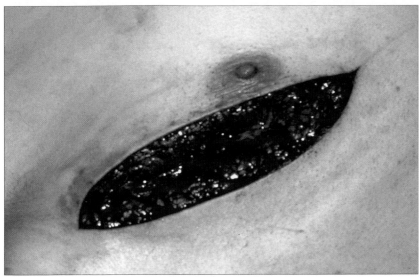

Surgical wound

Surgical incisions

 In surgery, linear incisions are made to gain access to underlying structures. These incisions are made under aseptic conditions and are associated with minimal surrounding tissue damage. Surgery on the open bowel may contaminate the access wound with gut bacteria. This increases the risk of a wound infection. After surgery, the everted skin edges are apposed with sutures. This minimises the soft tissue repair required.

Sutures 162

Wound complications

 A wound complication is defined as any event which adversely affects the healing process. Common complications affecting surgical wounds are:

- infection,
- haematoma,
- wound dehiscence,
- necrosis.

Infection 105
Haematoma 91
Dehiscence 107
Necrosis 140

Infection and haematoma predispose to wound dehiscence and necrosis. Both infection and haematoma cause swelling and an increase in tension in the sutured wound. This tension reduces the blood supply, leading to hypoxia, poor healing (allowing dehiscence) or tissue death (necrosis).

Sutures

 Insertion of sutures causes additional, though minor, trauma to tissues. The insertion points may form punctate scars. If the sutures have been tight, and have cut into encircled oedematous tissue, cross-hatched or "tramline" scars result. Increasingly, subcuticular sutures are being used to avoid this unsightly complication. However, greater skill is required to insert subcuticular sutures satisfactorily. Within the tissues, suture material acts as a foreign body and may become infected, producing an abscess or sinus.

Subcuticular G

Abscess 120 G
Sinus 137

113

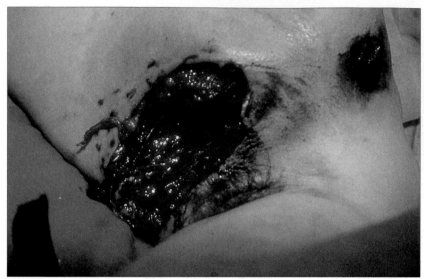

Shotgun injury of axilla.

The variety of penetrating injuries

A number of different agents can cause penetrating wounds. A knife may cause a small but deep wound, with possibly fatal internal damage. Shrapnel causes multiple, extensive injuries. Penetrating injuries are usually contaminated, increasing the risk of infection. They may contain foreign bodies, such as clothing, bullets or glass fragments. Animal and human bites are contaminated puncture wounds with a high risk of infection by oral organisms.

Gunshot wounds

A gunshot wound varies with the firearm and ammunition used. The effect depends on the number and type of projectiles and their impact velocity. In normal practice, low velocity injuries, such as embedded air-gun and shotgun pellets, are the most frequently seen. High velocity injuries, eg those caused by Armalite rifles, show extensive damage from absorption of large amounts of kinetic energy by the tissues around the bullet's track.

Management

The guiding principle of treating contaminated wounds is thorough debridement. All debris, whether foreign matter or dead tissue, must be removed before the wound can be closed. This may require much surgical expertise, especially following high velocity bullet wounds. For battlefield injuries, wound closure should be delayed until it is certain that no debris remains.

Gunshot

Debridement 161, 168

Blast or gunshot injuries. Haywood I, Skinner D. Br Med J 1990; 301: 1040-1042.

Avulsion and Crushing Injuries

Crushing and avulsion injuries differ from the wounds we have already described. These differences may make them difficult to treat.

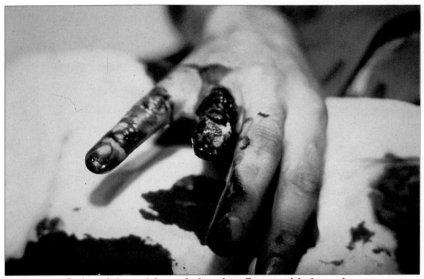

Industrial avulsion of the ring finger with bone loss.

Nature of injury

An avulsion injury results from tearing or forcible separation of tissues. It most often affects the extremities. Nerves, blood vessels and tendons can be stripped from the depth of the wound. Crushing injuries cause an area of cell death and vessel damage. Marked inflammation and swelling of the tissues typically follows and this can lead to increased tissue tension.

Inflammation 94

Causes of avulsion injury

Avulsion injuries can be seen following accidents with industrial or agricultural machinery. A household version is ring avulsion, where a force applied to a ring strips the finger of soft tissues.

Endothelial 92

Intimal G
Microsurgical

Outcome

Avulsion damages the endothelial lining of vessels an appreciable distance proximal to the level of tissue avulsion. Intimal damage is a potent stimulus to thrombosis. This makes microsurgical revascularisation or replantation of avulsed limbs and digits technically more difficult. Such procedures are much less likely to succeed than those involving sharp amputation injury.

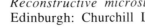

Reconstructive microsurgery. O'Brien B McC, Morrison W A. Edinburgh: Churchill Livingstone, 1987.

Shearing Injuries

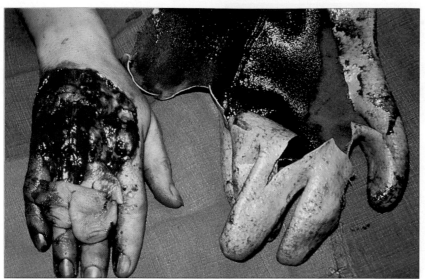

Industrial injury to the hand with degloving of the dorsal skin. Glove and skin flap have been peeled in a similar fashion.

Mechanism of damage

Vertically orientated vessels from the underlying fascia and muscles supply blood to the rich network of dermal capillaries. A natural tissue plane exists between skin and underlying structures such as muscle fascia or periosteum. Any force which strips or shears skin from underlying tissue may damage this blood supply and lead to devitalisation of the skin.

Degloving injury

An injury which results in separation of the skin from underlying tissue is called a degloving injury. It can occur in a number of ways and is seen following accidents involving machinery, or after road traffic accidents. The skin covering a limb which has been run over may appear almost undamaged. However, the shearing forces may have ruptured the vertically orientated blood vessels. Where this has occurred over an area wide enough to threaten skin viability, early recognition is essential. Prompt surgical intervention may allow some tissue to be salvaged.

Assessment of skin circulation

Skin colour and temperature give some indication of circulation within an area of skin. Press a finger tip on normal skin, eg the back of your hand, for a moment and then release it. A typical pattern and rate of blanching and re-perfusion occurs. Both the pattern and rate are altered by arterial or venous abnormalities. A fluorescein dye injection may also be used to define devitalised skin.

Dermis 84

116

Burns

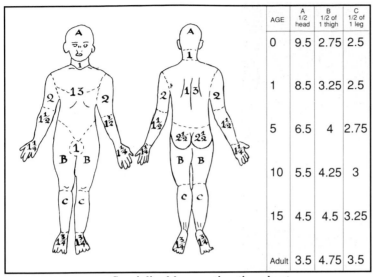

AGE	A ½ head	B ½ of 1 thigh	C ½ of 1 leg
0	9.5	2.75	2.5
1	8.5	3.25	2.5
5	6.5	4	2.75
10	5.5	4.25	3
15	4.5	4.5	3.25
Adult	3.5	4.75	3.5

Specialised burn estimation chart

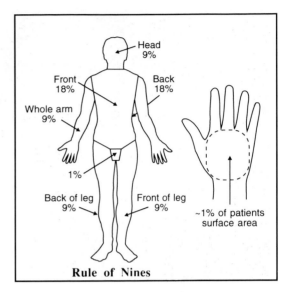

Rule of Nines

Causes of a burn

 Burns cause damage by coagulating cell proteins. A burn may be due to direct contact with flame, a heated object, or hot liquid (scald); or to radiation from a heat source. The passage of electric current through tissue or the application of noxious chemicals also causes injuries referred to as burns. They have similar consequences to thermal injuries but have some special features. Frostbite is caused by extreme cold that damages tissues especially vascular endothelium. The resulting thrombosis causes either tissue death or, on rewarming, leakage of protein and fluid through vessel walls.

Burn size

 Burns vary in severity. Minor burns tend to be of small area and superficial in depth. The severity of the burn increases when larger areas of skin are involved or when full thickness damage occurs. Area is expressed as a percentage of the body's total surface area. Simple rules for calculating this percentage (eg Rule of Nines or that the patient's palm represents 1% of his/her surface area) are useful during the initial management. Specialised burn estimation charts are then used to obtain accurate assessments of percentage area involved, especially in larger burns. There are different versions of these charts for children, which take into account the difference in body proportions with age.

Fluid replacement

 The size of the burn is important as it determines the volume of fluid which needs to be replaced during initial management. Fluid loss can be particularly dangerous in the young, due to their relatively small fluid reserves. Before the importance of fluid replacement was appreciated, many burns patients died of renal failure. Fluid loss starts soon after the injury and its rate is greatest in the first twelve hours.

Fluid replacement ABC of major trauma: Management of severe burns. Robertson C, Fenton O. Br Med J 1990; 301: 282.

Burns and their treatment. Muir I F K, Barclay T H, Settle J A D. London: Butterworth, 1987.

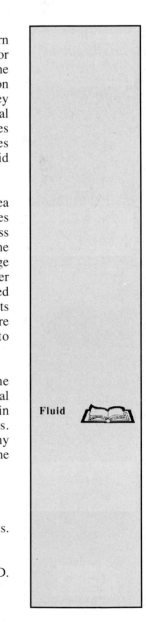

Fluid

Burn Depth

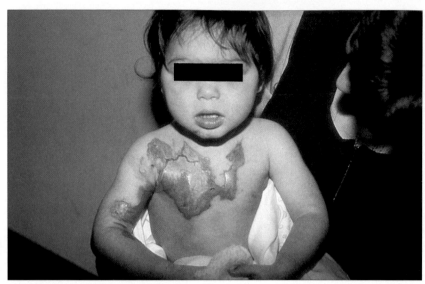

A child with a scald of the anterior chest.

The burn involving only the epidermis is, like the stage I pressure sore, a reaction to damage resulting in erythema. It is not included when calculating the area of a burn and is not considered further here.

Classification of burns

The depth of a burn is dependent on the temperature applied and the duration of exposure. Traditionally, burns were described in degrees but modern practice is to classify them, by thickness of damage, into three types:

- Superficial partial thickness - heals without scarring in most cases.
- Deep partial thickness - also known as deep dermal - heals but can result in significant scarring.
- Full thickness - always results in significant scarring.

The burn surface

Partial thickness burns usually blister. Copious amounts of fluid form beneath blisters. When the blister of a recent superficial partial thickness burn is ruptured, it reveals a uniform pink dermal surface. These burns are painful as the nerve endings of the dermis are viable. In contrast, when the blisters of deep dermal burns are burst or deroofed, a paler surface is revealed because the superficial vessels are coagulated. These wounds tend to be less painful because nerve endings are damaged.

A full thickness burn varies in appearance. It may look charred or abnormally pale in white skinned races. In dark skinned races there may be little obvious colour change from normal skin. Dermal nerve endings are destroyed so that pain is a less prominent feature. The full thickness burn feels leathery and appears depressed compared to surrounding skin. If circumferential, it may act as a tourniquet, causing pressure on underlying tissues. Compression can be relieved by a simple incision (escharotomy).

At risk groups

Many children are scalded each year by accidents in the home. The adventurous toddler is at risk from pulling a dangling kettle lead, spilling a cup of freshly made tea or coffee, or stepping into a hot bath to which cold water has yet to be added. Other groups of people particularly at risk from burns include epileptics, drug or alcohol abusers or others with impaired consciousness, the elderly, those suffering from psychiatric disorders, and those with diminished sensation.

ABC of child abuse: burns and scalds. Hobbs C J. Br Med J 1989; **298**: 1302.

Nerves 86

Eschartomy G

Scalded 85

Diminished sensation 86

Hazards of Burns

Burns may be associated with particular hazards which are described on this page.

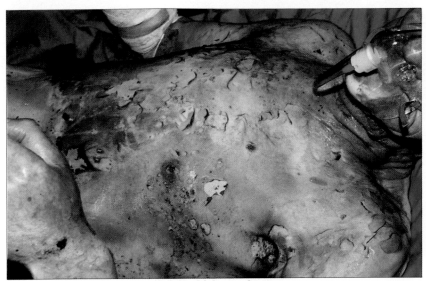

A full thickness burn.

How burns heal

 The treatment aim for a superficial uninfected burn is twofold: to protect it from mechanical damage and infection while providing a satisfactory environment for regeneration of the epithelium. Treatment of a full thickness burn is different. It can only heal, following debridement, by granulation and migration of epithelial cells from the periphery. This occurs at the rate of approximately 1 mm/week. A wound containing dead tissue, particularly in an immunocompromised host, is an ideal environment for infection. If the area of full thickness burn is large, taking several weeks to heal, the recommended treatment is early surgical excision and split skin grafting. This speeds debridement and resurfacing of the wound.

Regeneration 85
Full thickness 118
Debridement 161

Infection 105

Grafting 165

Life threatening events

 Patients who suffer burns may die from:
- smoke inhalation in a fire
- airway obstruction due to airway burn,
- fluid loss leading to renal failure,
- septicaemia, occurring in the later stages.

Inhalation injury in the lung leads to an alveolar diffusion defect which manifests at 24-48 hours. This may require artificial ventilation. The period of time which has elapsed since the burn is an important feature of the history.

Septicaemia 105, 172

Long term effects

 Deep partial thickness and full thickness burns cause permanent scarring. The appearance after skin grafting, though preferable to that following healing by secondary intent, is still not equivalent to normal skin. Scarring can have consequences for joint mobility, cosmetic appearance, psychological well-being and social development.

Problems relating to scarring in childhood include avoidance of school or specific activities which reveal the scars. There may be diminished self-esteem and loss of schooling through hospital attendance. Educational psychologists or child psychiatrists may be able to help. Adults may face employment related problems and interpersonal relationship difficulties.

Scarring 101, 129

Intent G 136

The treatment of burns. Cason J S. London: Chapman & Hall, 1987.
Complications of plastic surgery. Morris A McG, Stevenson J H and Watson A C H. London: Bailliere Tindall, 1989.

Wounds Resulting from Infection

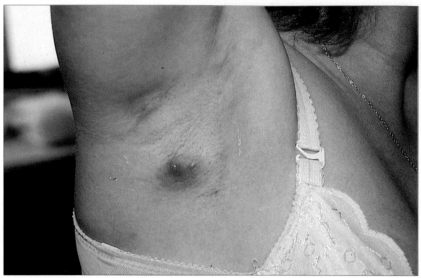

An axillary abscess.

Abscess formation

An abscess is a localised accumulation of pus, formed from white cells with necrosis and partial liquefaction of other cells and tissue. It is formed by complex interactions between the invading organism and the host defences. The infection becomes walled off by granulation tissue and a layer of dead white cells. Bacterial growth continues within the abscess until a certain concentration, dependent on the bacterial type, is reached (eg Staphylococcus aureus 10^9 per ml). Bacteria break down large sugar molecules, attracting fluid by osmosis. This increases the abscess size and internal pressure, producing pain.

Why incision is necessary

Localised skin and subcutaneous infections are common. They range from the simple boil (small skin abscess) to subcutaneous infections such as ischio-rectal abscesses. All present as acutely painful, red, hot swellings. The pus-filled centre becomes hypoxic and acidic, which slows bacterial growth. This environment is also unfavourable for macrophage function and lessens penetration of drugs. Thus bacteria remain alive within the abscess. Local environmental factors must change if the body is to eliminate the bacteria completely. The mainstay of treatment is surgical incision and drainage. An opening is made in the cavity, the pus evacuated and future drainage secured. Antibiotics serve only as an adjunct to surgery because they penetrate poorly into the abscess.

Necrotising infections

A number of rare skin infections give rise to areas of skin necrosis without abscess formation. Subcutaneous tissue destruction is caused by proliferation of synergic bacteria. Vascular thrombosis leads to skin necrosis. One of these rare infections is Fournier's gangrene (scrotal necrotising fasciitis). It is caused by mixed aerobic and anaerobic infection. When this type of infection occurs following laparotomy it is known as post-operative necrotising fasciitis. Only radical excision and vigorous and effective antibiotic therapy will stop the rapid spread of skin necrosis.

Abscess   128   G
Pus   105

Defences   97

Antibiotic   172   G

Synergic   G

Chronic Ulcers

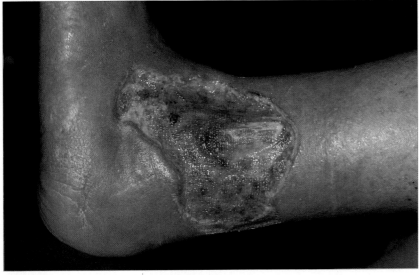

Chronic leg ulcer.

> "The cure of the part should not be attempted without treatment of the whole." Plato

Causes of chronicity

Chronic wounds form where a predisposing condition impairs the tissue's ability to maintain its integrity or heal damage. Common examples of such conditions are

- impaired venous drainage, e.g. venous hypertension,
- impaired arterial supply, e.g. peripheral vascular disease,
- metabolic abnormalities, e.g. diabetes mellitus, uraemia,
- persistent mechanical forces, e.g. pressure,
- neurogenic defects, e.g. leprosy
- . malignant disease, e.g. rodent ulcers,
- genetic disorders, e.g. sickle cell anaemia.

Assessment

Chronic ulcers require the same careful assessment as any other medical complaint. A thorough history and examination, followed by the relevant investigations, may reveal underlying conditions. The history may reveal symptoms of diabetes or peripheral vascular disease. Details of duration and previous treatment regimes suggest how the ulcer may be expected to respond to treatment. Investigations such as full blood count, blood biochemistry, blood sugar and liver function tests will reveal the presence of conditions which will adversely affect healing such as anaemia, uraemia, diabetes, jaundice or hypoproteinaemia.

Problem wounds are often the manifestation of an underlying condition combined with other adverse factors. An example of this might be an elderly patient with a leg ulcer, who smokes 50 cigarettes a day, has chronic bronchitis, severe peripheral vascular disease and a poor diet. Adverse factors which can be altered should be addressed in the treatment plan.

Hazards of compression treatment of the leg: an estimate from Scottish surgeons. Callam M J, Ruckley C V, Dale J J and Harper D R. Br Med J 1987; **295**: 1382.

Venous 123
Arterial 124

Diabetes 128
Pressure 125
Leprosy 86
Rodent ulcer G

History 112

Impaired Venous Drainage

Wound chronicity can result from longstanding impairment of venous drainage. This page deals with causes, manifestations and management of such impairment.

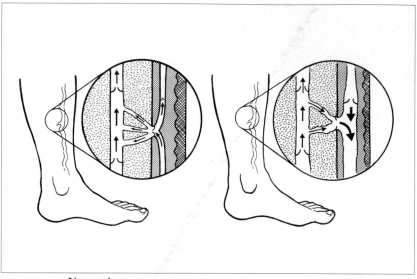

Normal   Abnormal

Venous drainage of the legs

The venous drainage of the leg is in two parts, the deep and superficial systems. Normally, during muscle relaxation, the superficial veins drain into the deep veins via perforating veins. These interconnections have one-way valves. Calf muscle contractions then help to pump the blood back to the heart via the deep venous system.

Venous hypertension

Damage to the venous valves of the legs may occur from a variety of causes, such as deep vein thrombosis or sustained venous hypertension (eg during pregnancy). Valvular incompetence leads to an abnormally high pressure in the superficial system. This manifests as varicose veins. Over time, characteristic microscopic changes (lipodermosclerosis) in the skin may develop. These include an increase in pigmentation, a loss of flexibility and fibrosis of the skin.

Treatment of varicose veins

Graduated compression stockings, injection therapy or surgery may be used to treat varicose veins. By applying external pressure to the veins, graduated compression stockings are thought to counteract abnormal internal pressures, making venous return to the heart more effective. Compression hosiery is available in several categories, depending on ability to retain predetermined levels of tension. Patients need follow-up to ensure their continued correct use of hosiery.

Deep vein thrombosis G

Varicose veins

Compression

ABC of vascular disease: varicose veins. Hobbs J T. Br Med J 1991; 303: 707.

Compression hosiery for stasis disorders. Anon. Drug Ther Bull 1982; 20 (21): 81-84.

Venous Ulceration

Venous hypertension of the lower limb may lead to venous ulceration. Where and why are explained here.

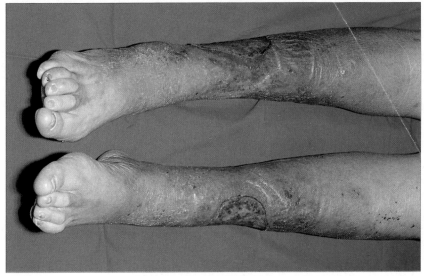

Venous ulcers of the leg.

It is estimated that 1-2% of the population of the UK suffers from leg ulcers. The NHS spends £300-600 million per year on the prevention and treatment of this condition.

Causative theories

 Established venous hypertension reduces the skin's ability to heal minor injuries. Chronic ulceration of the lower leg may result. The exact mechanisms are as yet poorly understood. The fibrin cuff theory postulates that venous hypertension results in increased small vessel permeability, allowing leakage of fibrinogen. Soluble fibrinogen then deposits as fibrin in the perivascular spaces. This acts as a barrier to diffusion and restricts vessel dilation. The more recent white cell trapping theory suggests that an accumulation of white cells with altered function may cause tissue damage.

Clinical aspects

 Venous ulceration occurs in the region of the ankle, especially above the medial malleolus, and may be accompanied by varicose eczema. These ulcers are irregular in shape and may be multiple. Pain may be present but is lessened by elevation and cooling. An increase in pain may herald infection and extension of ulceration. The patients are predominantly female, often overweight with a history of varicose veins and likely to have had recurrent ulcers.

Treatment

 In the UK the majority of venous ulcers are dressed by nurses in the community. Regular dressing, rest, elevation and weight loss are advised. The drug oxpentifylline combines enhancement of fibrinolysis and effects on white cells. Studies indicate it may be of benefit in venous ulceration when added to compression bandaging. Resistant or large ulcers can be skin grafted. This may heal the ulcer but there is a high recurrence rate. Where possible, the underlying venous hypertension should also be treated.

Venous ulcers. Allen S. Br Med J 1991; **300**: 826.

Chronic ulcer of the leg: clinical history. Callam M J, Harper D R, Dale J J and Ruckley C V. Lothian and Forth Valley leg ulcer study. Br Med J 1987; **294**: 1389-1391.

The cause of venous ulceration. Browse N L and Bernard K G. Lancet 1982; **ii**: 243-245.

White cell accumulation in dependent legs of patients with venous hypertension: a possible mechanism for trophic changes in the skin. Thomas P R S, Mash G B and Dormandy J A. Br Med J 1988; **296**: 1693-1695.

Oxpentifylline treatment of venous ulcers of the leg. Colgan M, Dormandy J A, Jones P W, Schraibman I G and Young R A L. Br Med J 1990; **300**: 972-975.

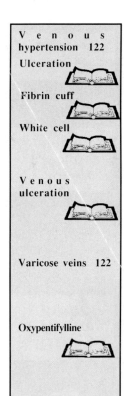

Arterial Insufficiency

The clinical features of another underlying cause of lower limb ulcers, arterial insufficiency, are described here.

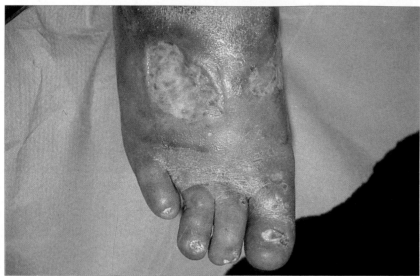

Dorsal foot ulcer, secondary to arterial disease, showing punched out nature.

Vascular responsiveness

 The blood vessels of the skin must be able to respond to the increased metabolic demands of injury, infection and healing. Any pathological process, such as atherosclerosis, which impairs this ability to respond can lead to tissue hypoxia and cell death. Even very minor injuries can result in skin breakdown and ulcer formation.

Peripheral vascular disease

Arterial ulcers are classically described as punched out and painful. They commonly affect the lower leg and foot, often occurring over bony prominences. They are sometimes associated with a history of intermittent claudication; absence of palpable pulses in the leg; cool, white, hairless skin and trophic changes in the nails. Measurement of perfusing pressures by Doppler ultrasound can give useful information about the tissue's blood flow and ability to heal. A brachial/popliteal pressure ratio of greater than 0.8 indicates that the blood supply to the region is satisfactory and the ulcer is not arterial in origin.

Other vascular causes

Venous insufficiency and atherosclerosis or a mixture account for the majority of lower limb ulcers. Around 5%, however, have other causes. Ulcers due to small vessel vasculitis, as is present in patients with rheumatoid arthritis, are among the most difficult ulcers to treat.

What measures are available which may lead to an increase in blood supply to a leg affected by peripheral vascular disease?

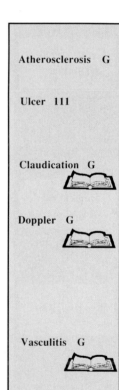

Atherosclerosis G

Ulcer 111

Claudication G

Doppler G

Vasculitis G

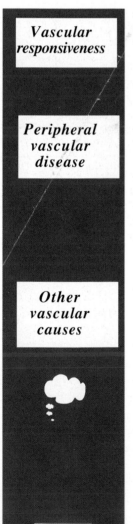 *Measurements of systolic pressure in the limbs of patients with arterial occlusive disease.* Bell G, Nielsen P E, Wolfson B et al.In: Surg Obstet 1973; **136**: 177-181.
Vasculitis and angiitis. In: Textbook of dermatology. Rook A, Wilkinson DS, Ebling F J G et al (eds). Oxford: Blackwell, 1986.

Pressure Sores

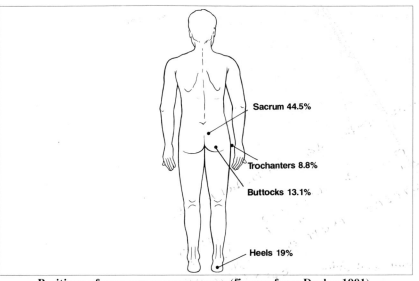

Positions of common pressure sores (figures from Dealey 1991)

Sacrum 44.5%
Trochanters 8.8%
Buttocks 13.1%
Heels 19%

You can put anything on a pressure sore except the patient.

Causal factors

 Pressure sores are caused by ischaemia due to unrelieved pressure over bony points. There are often other contributing factors. Shear and friction may occur when a patient is slid up the bed. The presence of moisture, particularly relevant when the patient is incontinent, leads to maceration of the skin. Faecal soiling results in bacterial and chemical contamination of the skin. For the continent patient lying on even a soft mattress, two hours is generally taken as the maximum that skin can tolerate the effects of pressure without risk of damage.

At risk groups

 Unrelieved pressure most commonly occurs when an individual is bed or chair bound. The elderly, sick, debilitated or paralysed are particularly at risk because they tend to be immobile and may not be able to move themselves to relieve pressure. Those with a neuological defect are also at risk of developing sores due to lack of sensory feedback. However, pressure sores can develop in any individual when the skin is subjected to unrelieved pressure. Common sites are:

- the ischial region — in the chair bound
- the posterior aspect of the heel ⎫
- the sacral prominence ⎬ — in the supine position
- the trochanteric region — in the lateral position.

Sores may develop over any other prominence given sustained pressure, eg lateral aspect of the knee, following the poor application of a plaster cast or use of an ill fitting prosthesis; or the medial aspect of the knee following pressure from the other knee.

Contamination G

Trochanteric G

 Pressure sores: clinical practice and scientific approaches. Bader D (ed) London: Macmillan, 1989.

The size of the pressure sore problem in a teaching hospital. Dealey C. Journal of Advanced Nursing, 1991: 16: 663-670.

Pressure Sore Classification

This page deals with pressure sore classification, an aid to prognosis and management.

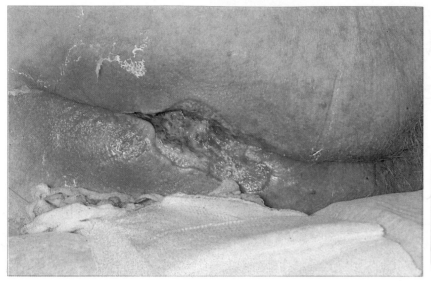

Necrotic sacral sore

"Know your enemy"

Stage and depth

 Pressure sores are divided into four types, according to depth. The first two involve the skin only.

- The **first stage** is more accurately described as a pressure effect. The skin is not broken but reacts to injury becoming red and inflamed.
- In a **second stage** sore, the epidermis, and possibly some of the dermis, become necrotic causing a deficiency in the skin cover.
- **Stage three** sores involve subcutaneous tissue.
- **Stage four** lesions penetrate underlying muscle or bone.

Continued pressure results in an ever deepening sore. Subcutaneous fat is more sensitive to pressure than the overlying skin. Sores are frequently flask shaped, consisting of a large cavity undermining surrounding skin.

Deep sores can be initiated by primary necrosis of underlying tissues, especially subcutaneous fat. This leads to secondary skin breakdown. Pressure induced ischaemia is a factor but shearing of the subcutaneous layers in relation to a fixed bony point is thought to be important. Clinically this is seen as an initial inflammation of the skin, which develops into a black plaque and then separates, releasing a foul smelling discharge.

Management of deeper sores

Stage three and four pressure sores often have large amounts of necrotic tissue deep within the wound cavity. This is difficult to debride. The extensive nature of the cavity dictates that, even when the wound is fully debrided, granulation and eventual epithelialisation of the wound will take many weeks or months. Plastic surgery techniques may achieve earlier healing.

Pressure sores. Ward A B. Prescribers' Journal 1990; 30(6): 253-264.

Pressure sores

Subcataneous fat 82

Necrosis 140

Shearing 116

Prevention of Pressure Sores

Measures for prevention of pressure sores are introduced, and their resource implications discussed.

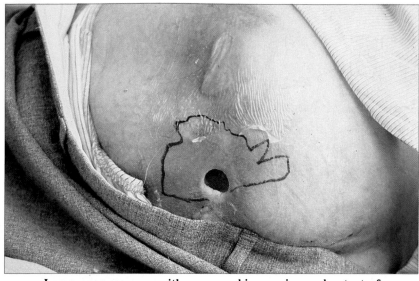

Large pressure sore with narrow skin opening and extent of undermining outlined.

Most pressure sores are preventable - given adequate resources, proper prophylactic procedures, and trained staff.

Scoring systems

Pressure sores cause much misery and contribute to mortality. The first stage in prevention is to identify those at risk. A number of scoring systems can be used, such as those of Norton and Waterlow. Additional preventive measures can then be taken.

Preventive measures

The first essential of prevention (and treatment) is the avoidance of prolonged pressure. The provision of a handhold above the head of the bed helps patients to lift themselves more easily, relieving pressure. Frequent turning of immobile patients, every two hours or more often, with inspection of susceptible areas is a simple routine measure. This, combined with good nursing practice when lifting patients and caring for the incontinent, can prevent problems developing. A number of special beds, mattresses and cushions have been developed to help relieve and redistribute pressure. These range from the relatively simple and inexpensive, such as overlay mattresses, through mattresses with alternating inflating and deflating segments, to expensive air-beds. Independent chair bound individuals should be advised to lift themselves every 15 minutes or so, using an alarm or charts as necessary.

Cost implications

The treatment of established pressure sores is costly and labour intensive. The UK National Health Service spends an estimated £350 million annually on this largely preventable condition. The prevalence of pressure sores in hospital ranges from 4 to 9% in UK studies. In the USA, it is estimated that 1 million Americans are treated for pressure sores every year, at a hospitalisation cost of $2,000-30,000 per patient.

A risk assessment card. Waterlow J. Nursing Times 1985: **81(48)**: 49-55.

Aids to prevent pressure sores. Young J B. Br Med J 1990; **300**: 1002.

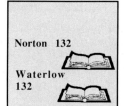

Norton 132

Waterlow 132

Metabolic Defects

A fourth major cause of ulcers is diabetes mellitus. Its adverse effects on healing are explored here.

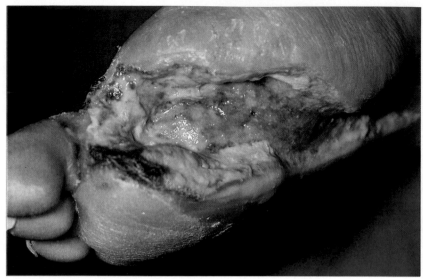

Ulceration of the foot in a diabetic patient

"A little neglect may breed mischief." Benjamin Franklin

How diabetes affects healing

 Diabetes mellitus adversely affects the healing of skin wounds in a number of ways that are cumulative in their effects.

- Diabetics have a five-fold risk of wound infections.
- The inflammatory response is impaired and granulation tissue may form poorly.
- Diabetes is associated with the development of atherosclerosis. The effects may be exacerbated by small vessel disease, a thickening of the capillary basement membrane. Even though a diabetic patient may have palpable foot pulses, small vessel disease can impair blood flow and healing.
- The peripheral nerves are damaged by vascular impairment, which diminishes proprioception and pain sensation.

Advice for diabetics

 The feet of a diabetic are particularly susceptible to injury, infection and chronic wound formation. Seemingly innocuous breaks in the skin can result in severe infections. Meticulous attention to the condition of the feet is essential and allows early treatment of any problem. Rest, elevation, good control of blood sugar levels and prompt treatment with systemic antibiotics are required for seemingly minor injuries. If injuries are neglected, extensive abscess formation and even osteomyelitis can occur with little inflammatory response or pain.

Scale of the problem

 The prevalence of diabetes mellitus in the UK is estimated as 1-2% of population. It is estimated that there are 11 million diabetics in the USA. In 1980, US hospital costs for diabetes related peripheral vascular disease were quoted as $200 million.

The diabetic foot. Boulton A J M. Med Clin of N Am 1988; **72**(6): 1513-1530.

Diabetes G

Nerves 86

Feet

Abscess 120
Osteomyelitis G

Malignancy

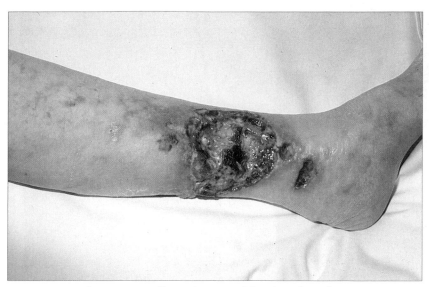

Squamous cell carcinoma arising in a leg ulcer.

Skin neoplasia

 The integrity of the skin's surface can be interrupted by a neoplastic lesion. This may be a primary tumour arising in the skin, an invasive growth arising in underlying tissues or metastatic spread from a distant tumour. A long-standing ulcer or old burn scar may give rise to squamous cell carcinoma.

Marjolin's ulcer

 Marjolin described ulceration due to squamous cell carcinoma arising in a burn scar. Squamous cell carcinoma associated with a long history of ulceration of the lower leg is often called a Marjolin's ulcer. Diagnosis of the true nature of the ulcer is often delayed. Close inspection will reveal little sign of healing, heaped up margins and abnormal granulations. Secondary amyloidosis is also a potential complication of any long-standing ulcer, irrespective of aetiology. Biopsy of all such ulcers should be considered, to exclude these rare but important conditions.

Prevalence

 Up to 2% of ulcers seen at specialist clinics are skin cancers. Early referral of atypical non-healing ulcers for biopsy is essential. Certain systemic conditions, mycosis fungoides or chronic arsenic poisoning, are also characterised by multiple skin malignancies. Similarly, genetic abnormalities such as xeroderma pigmentosa are associated with multiple ulcerative tumours of the skin.

Marjolin G

Ulcere. Marjolin J N. Dictionnaire de Med 1828; 21: 31.

Iatrogenic Causes

Drugs may hinder healing. Iatrogenic causes, including radiation, must be remembered in the aetiology of ulcers.

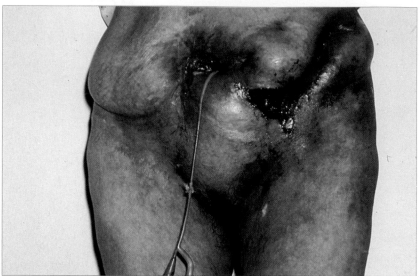

Endarteritis obliterans, telangiectasia and poor healing caused by radiotherapy.

Steroids

A number of medical treatments have unwanted effects which can affect healing. Many drugs hinder one or more of the processes of healing. Steroids affect all the stages. Impairment is greatest if the steroid was administered at, or before, the time of the injury, suggesting its greatest effect is on inflammation. Steroids block the release of histamine. Glucocorticoids stabilise the lysosomal membranes, preventing the release of active substances. They also reduce the release of arachidonic acid and its derivatives.

Treatment of malignancy

Impaired healing is often a problem when treating malignant disease. The adverse effects of malignancy on healing may be compounded by the administration of cytotoxic drugs. These interfere with cell replication and impair healing. Radiotherapy, which suppresses the immune system, can further aggravate matters. Irradiation also has marked effects on the skin. These may manifest immediately after treatment as a dermatosis. Many years after radiotherapy, reduced vascularity and fibrosis are associated with poor healing and risk of skin breakdown.

Medical accidents

In addition to the recognised complications of some therapies, occasional medical accidents can result in a wound. For example, a burn may result from a diathermy pad if proper care is not taken. The extravascular injection of drugs, especially cytotoxic mixtures, can lead to necrosis of overlying skin. Extravasation of a solution, for example, sodium bicarbonate during emergency resuscitation, may also result in skin loss.

Iatrogenic G

Histamine 94

Arachidonic G

Radiotherapy

Immune system G

Effects of radiation on cells. Gillies N E. Br Med J 1987; 295: 1390.

State of Mind

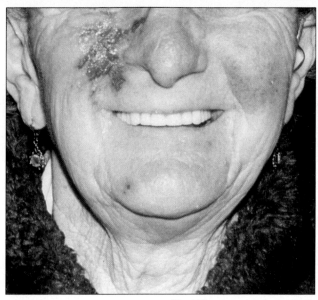 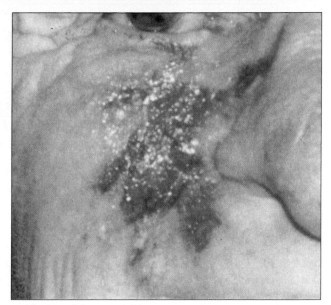

Factitious wound: a facial wound caused by scratching.

Mind over matter

Psychological states of mind seem to influence wound healing processes. The exact mechanisms are difficult to determine. It is postulated that the mechanisms are indirect, via an effect on the immune system or sleep patterns. Anxiety has well recognised effects on skin blood flow, but any relationship this may have to healing is unexplored. Hypnotism and traditional Chinese medicine, used in some societies, have been shown to reduce inflammation. Depression may lead to inadequate nutrition and self-care. Very occasionally, wounds are self-inflicted.

Factitious wounds

Factitious wounds are maintained by repeated minor self-trauma, because the patient perceives the wound as beneficial. Healing is prevented by the direct physical interference of the patient, although this is denied. There may be a valid history of trauma originally, but the wound fails to heal normally or may extend. This is an extremely difficult diagnosis to make. A chronic wound with a geometric or angular shape and no complicating factors should arouse suspicion. Psychiatric treatment is of benefit and may result in wound healing.

Social isolation

In large studies of leg ulcers, 1-2% frustrate all attempts to achieve healing. The wound may become the patient's passport to attention. The formation of leg ulcer clubs has been suggested, to provide the social support that is often lacking in these individuals' lives.

The elderly are particularly likely to become socially isolated. Specialist community health visitors for the elderly are increasing in number in the UK. Patients may be eligible for meals on wheels, a domestic help or referral to a day centre. Encouragement to maintain social and family contacts should be given.

Nutrition 106

131

Norton and Waterlow Scoring Systems

Waterlow Pressure Risk Assessment
Ring Score in Table, add total to special risk scores
(Several scores per category can be used.)

Build/Weight for Height		Visual Skin Type Risk Areas		Continence		Mobility		Sex/Age		Appetite	
Average	0	Healthy	0	Complete	0	Fully Mobile	0	Male	1	Average	0
						Restricted/ Difficult	1				
Above Average	2	Tissue Paper	1	Occasional Incont.	1	Restless/ Fidgety	2	Female	2	Poor	1
Below Average	3	Dry	1	Cath/incont. Faeces	2	Apathetic	3	14-49	1	Anorexic	2
		Odematous	1	Doubly Incont	3	Inert/ Traction	4	50-64	2		
		Clammy	1					65-74	3		
		Discolour	2					75-80	4		
		Broken/Spot	3					81 +	5		

Special Risks		
1) Poor Nutrition, e.g. Terminal Cachexia	8	
2) Sensory Deprivation, e.g. Diabetes, Paraplegia, CVA	5	
3) High Dose Anti-inflammatory or Steroids in use	3	
4) Smoking 10 + per day	1	
5) Orthopaedic Surgery/Fracture below waist	5	

Total Score =

Assessment Value

At Risk	=	10
High Risk	=	15
Very High Risk	=	20

Norton score, for assessing degree of risk of developing pressure sores, developed for use with elderly patients. Score of ≤14 indicates vulnerability to pressure sores and score of ≤ 12 high risk.

Physical state		Mental state		Activity	
Good	(4)	Alert	(4)	Ambulant	(4)
Fair	(3)	Apathetic	(3)	Walks with help	(3)
Poor	(2)	Confused	(2)	Chairbound	(2)
Very bad	(1)	Stuporous	(1)	Bedbound	(1)

Mobility		Incontinence	
Full	(4)	None	(4)
Slightly limited	(3)	Occasional	(3)
Very limited	(2)	Usually urine	(2)
Immobile	(1)	Double	(1)

Section 5
Form: Size, Shape and State of Skin Wounds

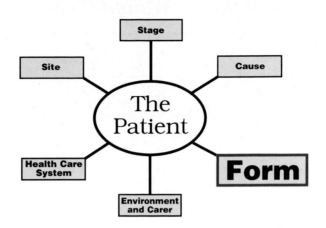

The Wound Organiser

Having explored the influence of cause, the Organiser next highlights the form of the wound and what this implies for healing.

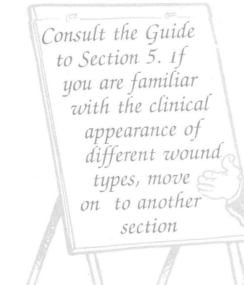

Consult the Guide to Section 5. If you are familiar with the clinical appearance of different wound types, move on to another section

Guide to Section 5

Clinical Manifestation: Wound Types

Type and Examples	Appearances	Needs of wound
Incised Surgical incision. Traumatic wound from broken glass.	Surgical incisions are straight, vertical, clean. Trauma may produce ragged edges.	Apposition of wound edges.
Sinus/Fistula Sinus tract due to suture. Fistula in ano.	Discharges pus. Discharges exudate or pus.	Treatment of underlying cause, then as for cavity wound.
Cavity Surgical excision. Incised abcess. Tissue loss.	Full thickness wound. Adjacent skin may be undermined.	Drainage Absorption of exudate. Promotion of granulation, followed by epithelialisation.
Flat Abrasion. Granulating wound.	Wound surface may be epidermis, dermis, subcutaneous or granulation tissue.	Protection. Promotion of epithelialisation.
Necrotic Any wound containing dead tissue due to initial injury or complications.	Dead skin may be hard, dry and black. Dead connective tissue may appear grey.	Removal of necrotic material. Promotion of granulation and epithelialisation.
Infected Wound caused by infection, e.g. abscess. Any wound which becomes infected.	An inflamed wound. Presence of pus.	Drainage and debridement. Eradication of infection, then as for uninfected wound.

Clinical Appearances

"Everything that happens, happens as it should, and if you observe carefully, you will find this to be so." Marcus Aurelius Antoninus (121-180 AD)

What to look for

 Inspection of the wound provides information on the five "S"s

- size,
- shape,
- state,
- site,
- stage of healing.

In previous sections, site and stage of healing were discussed. Here the size, shape and state of the wound provide a further point in the Wound Organiser - the form.

What **size** is the wound? Are there hidden extensions? Size affects the amount of repair necessary. A large area of full thickness wound requires a significant amount of time to heal, and might be referred for surgery. A small area heals more rapidly and can be managed conservatively.

What **shape** is the wound? This affects the type of tissues involved and the ease of management. Cavity wounds can contain necrotic tendon and bone at the base. Access may be difficult.

What is the **state** of the wound? Is it contaminated, infected or clean?

Organiser 77

Cavity 138

Infected 141

 The skin. In: Clinical examination. Macleod J, Munro J (eds). Edinburgh: Churchill Livingstone, 1986: 85-95.

Incised Wounds

Incised ←
Sinus
Fistula
Cavity

Flat
Necrotic
Infected

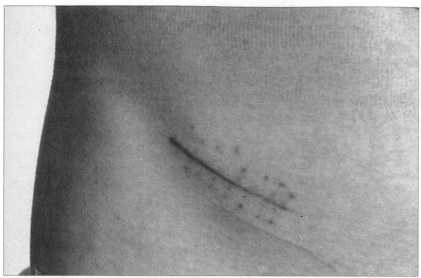

Healing appendicectomy wound.

Cuts and lacerations

Surgical incisions have clean-cut vertical edges. Traumatic incisions often produce wound edges that are undercut, irregular or contaminated. When skin is cut, the wound edges retract. The skin's natural elasticity, combined with swelling, gives a gaping wound and the appearance of missing skin. Traumatic lacerations may be associated with damage to underlying structures and this should be ascertained prior to treatment.

Freshly incised wounds should be cleaned and the edges apposed with sutures. Healing occurs by first intention (primary healing). For heavily contaminated wounds or wounds over 12 hours old, suturing may be delayed until the risk of infection is reduced. This is called delayed primary suture and is usually performed at about five days. Otherwise the gap is allowed to heal by second intention (secondary healing).

Suturing

Sutures are used to appose and evert the wound edges. This gives maximum contact and minimum space within the wound. In an uncomplicated wound, epithelialisation may occur within 48 - 72 hours.

Complications of a sutured wound

It is important that haemostasis is adequate, so that blood does not accumulate within the wound. Excess clot (haematoma) delays healing and may be associated with subsequent infection and wound breakdown.

When should sutures be removed?

The time for which sutures should be left in a wound is a matter of judgement. Only general guidelines can be suggested. The blood supply to the area, the tension and movement to which the wound is subject due to its site, the age and condition of the patient, and cosmetic factors all need to be balanced. Facial wounds will normally have developed sufficient strength by four to five days for the sutures to be removed, lessening their cosmetic impact. Wounds on the limbs or trunk require support for longer and sutures are retained for ten days or more.

Surgical 113

Elasticity 84

Primary 93

Secondary 93

Sutures 162

Haematoma 91

Age 107

136

Sinuses and Fistulae

Incised
Sinus ←
Fistula ←
Cavity

Flat
Necrotic
Infected

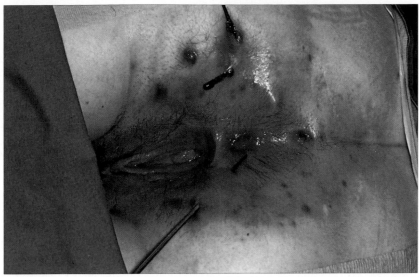

Multiple perianal tracts in a patient with Crohn's disease. Upper probe demonstrates a sinus, lower probe a fistula.

If the full extent of the wound cannot be seen, its true nature will be unknown until it is investigated.

Causes

 A sinus is a blind tract which opens onto an epithelial surface. A fistula is an abnormal tract connecting two epithelial surfaces. Before embarking on treatment of any tract, the cause must be investigated. A sinus will often indicate the presence of a deep chronic discharging abscess or infected material beneath the surface. This material may be implanted foreign matter or dead tissue. Fistulae may be due to infection, trauma, iatrogenic causes, malignancy or inflammatory bowel disease. Sinuses and fistulae may be congenital in origin. A common cause of a sinus is infection around a buried, non-absorbable suture. Less commonly, multiple sinuses are seen in chronic osteomyelitis, where they are associated with the presence of dead bone.

Crohn's disease

Patients with Crohn's disease may present with recurrent perianal infection, which leads to fistula and sinus formation. These tracts are difficult to treat while the disease is still active. Of patients with Crohn's disease, 60% will, at some time, experience this complication.

Hidradenitis suppurativa

 In the condition of hidradenitis suppurativa, an abnormality of apocrine sweat glands predisposes to blockage of the glands and to skin abscess and tract formation in the axilla, groin and perineum.

Pilonidal sinus

 Pilonidal sinus is a condition arising in post-pubertal hair-bearing skin, especially when subjected to maceration, repeated friction and pressure. The natal cleft is the commonest site. Traditionally, the occurrence of pilonidal sinus was said to be linked to occupations involving jeep driving, horse riding, etc, and to affect the finger clefts in barbers. However, now, about half the cases appear to have none of these occupational factors and about half occur in females.

Treatment

 Having removed the underlying cause of a sinus, the wound may be treated with dressings which encourage healing from the depth, as for a cavity. A fistula tract may have to be laid open or excised. Where this would damage essential structures, eg fistula in ano, treatment is more complicated. When treatment of a fistula or sinus tract is incomplete, recurrence can be expected.

Iatrogenic G

Crohn's disease G

137

Cavity Wounds

Incised
Sinus
Fistula
Cavity

Flat
Necrotic
Infected

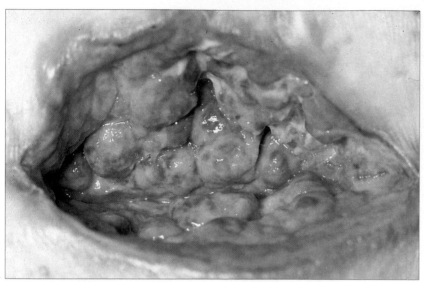

Cavity wound following a surgical excision.

Causes

Wounds in the form of a cavity develop following deep tissue loss, which may be traumatic, infective, due to pressure or following surgery. Healing requires the removal of any residual dead tissue, the promotion of granulation to fill the defect and the maintenance of free drainage of all parts of the wound. Areas loculated by the healing process are predisposed to infection.

Infective 120
Pressure 126

Care

Packing cavity wounds debrides, or simply keeps the wound surfaces clean and apart. It maintains good drainage by absorption and allows the granulation tissue to form 'from the bottom up'. Excessive packing can delay healing by local pressure on the tissues and interference with wound drainage. Cavities, especially if infected, produce significant amounts of exudate from their linings. Therefore absorbent dressings are required. Materials in use as cavity fillers all have some absorptive capacity and include gauze, polysaccharide beads, alginates, hydrogels, foams and hydrocolloid pastes.

Granulation 98

Gauze G
Alginates G
Silicone foam G
Polysaccharide
  beads G

Surgical management

Extensive cavities, for instance those associated with pressure sores, require a considerable time to heal. The option of surgical treatment should be considered. Healthy, well vascularised tissue can be brought in to fill the defect and speed healing. Large cutaneous or composite musculocutaneous flaps may be fashioned to cover the affected area.

Flaps G

Plastic Surgery: Pressure Sores. Grabb W G and Smith W. Boston: Little, Brown, 1990.

Flat Wounds

Incised
Sinus
Fistula
Cavity

Flat
Necrotic
Infected

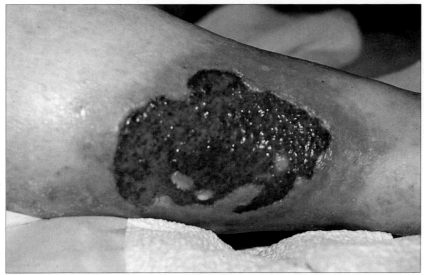

Flat granulating wound

Causes

 Flat wounds can develop as a deep wound heals. They are also created by a number of different agents, some of which remove tissue (eg an abrasion) while others devitalise the tissue in situ (eg a full thickness burn).

Burn 118

Is it crusted or necrotic?

 Flat wounds present in various guises. A flat granulating surface is seen when a deep wound is healing or in a chronic ulcer. A white or charred surface of dead tissue is formed following a full thickness burn. Crusting occurs when an abrasion is left uncovered. When wounds are kept moist, various appearances are evident, dependent on depth of damage.

Granulating 98

Ulcer 111

Does it need grafting?

 A large flat wound may be resurfaced by transplantation of part of the epidermal layer of the skin from another site. This technique is known as split skin grafting. The graft will survive if placed on clean viable tissues, such as a fresh wound bed or on granulation tissue. It will not survive well over relatively avascular areas, such as bare bone or bare tendon. Survival is decreased by the presence of dead tissue, fibrinous deposits or infection. The donor site heals by regeneration.

Grafting

Regeneration 85

ABC of plastic surgery. Davies D. London: British Medical Journal, 1985.

Necrotic Wounds

Incised
Sinus
Fistula
Cavity

Flat
Necrotic
Infected

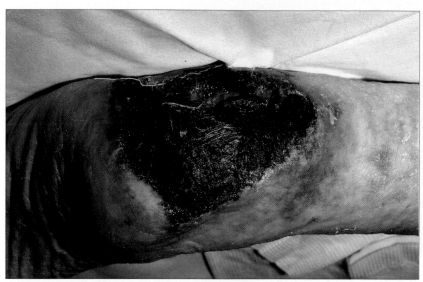

Black necrotic tissue lying within a wound.

> Dead tissue cannot be revitalised, but inappropriate care of a wound can lead to further tissue death.

Causes

Dead tissue appears in a wound for a number of reasons. It may result from the original insult or may have developed subsequently. A suture, too tightly tied, can strangulate the tissue it encompasses, especially if there is marked wound oedema. Similarly, if wound edges are apposed under too much tension, the blood supply is decreased and necrosis may result. Infection is another potent cause of tissue death.

Natural progression

Initially, the cause governs the appearance of devitalised tissue. Later, it may form into a black, hard eschar. Dry at first, with time this may soften by autolysis and bacterial liquefaction. It is eventually shed as slough. The presence of dead tissue in a wound delays healing.

Blunt injury may leave the skin surface intact, while damaging vessels and fat beneath the skin. This may cause a subcutaneous haematoma or fat necrosis. Subcutaneous haematoma may increase skin tension and vessel damage reduces skin blood supply. Necrosis may then occur and healing may be delayed until the haematoma and eschar are removed or separate naturally.

Dead tissue 96

Eschar G

Infected Wounds

Incised
Sinus
Fistula
Cavity

Flat
Necrotic
Infected ←

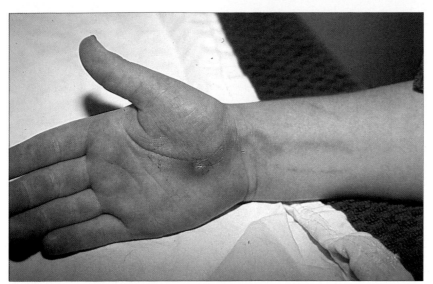

An infected wound with lymphangitis

Appearance

 Infection of a wound causes an intense inflammatory reaction and tissue destruction. The skin becomes red, hot and shiny. Pus may be present. Fluid, debris and organisms in the tissues are drained by the lymphatics, which may also become inflamed. This lymphangitis manifests as a red line running from the wound towards the regional lymph nodes. These in turn may become swollen and painful (lymphadenitis).

Consequences of infection

A wound infection may result in release of bacteria into the bloodstream (bacteraemia), and more widespread infection. Infected skin wounds of the central area of the face drain via lymphatics into intracranial veins. Rarely this may cause thrombosis of the cavernous sinus.

Prevention and cure

 Wound management aims to prevent infection by a number of measures:

- remove dead tissue in which bacteria may thrive,
- remove organisms by cleansing,
- preclude entry of bacteria by dressings,
- administer prophylactic antibiotics.

Once an infection is diagnosed, treatment consists of:
- appropriate antibiotic therapy,
- measures to provide free drainage of the wound,
- removal of any foreign material.

Lymphatic channels

The lymphatic system is a series of endothelial lined channels. These drain excess tissue fluid via regional lymph nodes, into the venous circulation. The system's chief function is the clearance of protein and other macromolecules, which are carried by the extracellular fluid and some lymphocytes. Fluid may accumulate in the tissues either from an excess of capillary filtrate, as in inflammation, or from reduced drainage due to defective or absent lymphatics.

Remove dead
  tissue 161, 168
Cleansing   160
Dressings   164
Prophylaxis 172

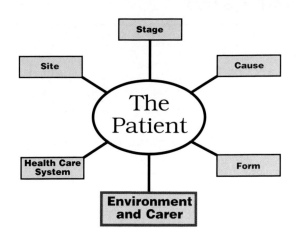

The Wound Organiser

Working round the Organiser we now look at how external environment, for patient and carer, influences wound healing and management.

Should the patient be admitted to hospital? Read Section 6 to find out

Guide to Section 6

Environment and Carers

Environment and Carers	Implications	Indications and Examples
Teaching hospital Specialist units and teams.	Maximum expertise and facilities. Constant availability. Maximum cost. Maximum disruption of patient's lifestyle.	**Wounds requiring specialist management** • Major wounds. • Minor wounds associated with other major problems • Wounds with complications.
District hospital General surgical and medical teams .	High level of expertise and facilities. Constant availability. Visiting specialists.	**Wounds requiring hospital facilities** • Major wounds. • Minor wounds associated with other health problems. • Wounds with complications.
Cottage hospital Supervised by GP. General nursing care.	Constant nursing and domestic care. Intermittent advice.	**Wounds not requiring full hospital facilities** • Patients recovering from major wounds. • Minor wounds with other health problems.
Nursing home Variable nursing experience. GP visits.	Domestic care. Intermittent nursing care. Intermittent advice.	**Wounds not requiring hospital facilities** • Less severe wounds in patients with additional problems.
Residential care Community nurse visits. GP visits.	Domestic care. Intermittent nursing care. Intermittent advice. Cost effective.	**Wounds not requiring hospital facilities** • Minor wounds in elderly or disabled.
Sheltered housing Community nurse visits. GP visits.	Supervised own domestic care. Intermittent care and advice.	**Wounds not requiring hospital facilities** • Minor wounds in elderly or disabled.
GP surgery Surgery nurse. Nurse practitioner. GP.	Cost effective. Minimal disruption to lifestyle. Patient visits facilities and carers.	**Wounds not requiring hospital facilities** • Minor wounds in mobile patients. • Post operative wounds. • Healing major wounds.
Patient's home Community nurse visits. GP visits.	Cost effective. Little disruption to lifestyle. Few facilities. Intermittent advice and care or self-care.	**Wounds not requiring hospital facilities** • Minor or healing wounds in patients with limited mobility.
At work Occupational nursing and medica specialists.	Cost effective. Specialist knowledge of work environment.	**Wounds not requiring hospital facilities** • First aid for accidents at work. • Minor wounds in patients continuing to work.
Site of accident Bystander or no care. Paramedic/ambulance team. Mobile hospital team or GP.	Few facilities. Variable expertise in first aid.	**Immediate treatment**. • Any accidental injury.

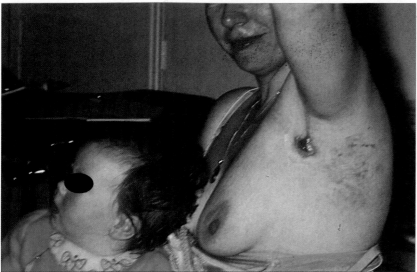

This mother continues to care for her child while her wound is treated.

A realistic treatment plan

 People live in a wide variety of environments and social circumstances. These affect how much the patient's behaviour can be modified, what treatments are practical, what facilities are available and who will manage the wound. An important part of management is the assessment and, if necessary, modification of environmental factors to facilitate treatment. The final treatment plan must take into account those environmental and behavioural factors which cannot be modified.

Adjustment of lifestyle

 Most patients will agree to adjust their lifestyles temporarily, to accommodate the presence of a wound. Compliance is improved by clear explanations of the reasons for advice. Other patients need assistance; either suggestions, provision of services or a change in environment. The family, neighbours and friends are a powerful resource that may need to be mobilised. For instance, a mother with small children will be unable to follow advice to rest at home unless another adult can take on her child-minding and domestic chores. Some patients refuse to adjust. This last group is difficult to help and often frustrating to treat.

Money and wounds

 Wounds have financial implications - in time lost from work, an inability to return to the same work or a permanent disability. The self-employed or casually employed risk losing their livelihood. This is a source of considerable anxiety and may lead to non-compliance. The patient may be eligible to claim industrial injury compensation for work related injuries or criminal injury compensation. A knowledge of the various sources of financial advice will enable the patient to be helped through a difficult time. The Welfare Benefits team in the local Social Work Department can advise on this.

Behaviour 146

Compensation 102

Benefits

Benefits for people incapable of work. Ennals S. Br Med J 1991; **302**: 160.

Industrial benefits. Ennals S. Br Med J 1991; **302**: 400.

Behaviour Patterns

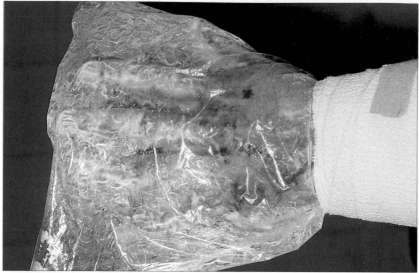

A plastic bag dressing isolates the wound while allowing movement.

> "Then we must consider the patient - his mode of life, his mannerisms, his silences, his thoughts, his habits of sleep and his dreams." Hippocrates

Advice

Patients require information on how their behaviour will affect healing, which patterns are beneficial and which detrimental. For example, oedema delays healing and predisposes to joint stiffness. Elevation of the injured part encourages drainage of excess fluid via the lymphatics. Patients with leg wounds are advised to sit with their feet raised above hip level and those with hand injuries to keep the hand elevated (eg in a high sling). Exercise may disrupt wound surfaces and therefore resting an injured part is recommended. In certain circumstances, however, eg an adult patient with a burned hand, the combination of oedema and immobility leads to joint stiffness. To avoid this, early mobilisation, usually supervised by a physiotherapist, is encouraged. Advice must be tailored for the injury and the individual.

Changes in environment

Decisions, on whether the patient should remain at home, continue to work, return to work after injury, be admitted for care, or be discharged from hospital, all depend on the individual's circumstances as well as the state of the wound. Occupations where the wound may become contaminated with substances such as oil or chemicals, or where adequate rest is not possible, should be avoided. Resumption of work may be good physiotherapy, provided consideration is given to safety if machinery or other hazards are involved. A return to work before healing is complete is often practicable, though it may be prohibited for some patients, particularly those dealing with food.

Permanent changes

Injury can have long term sequelae. Permanent disability may prevent a return to previous employment and may require retraining and support. Psychological effects, eg post traumatic stress disorder, agoraphobia, depression or personality changes, may complicate recovery. Cosmetic deformities exacerbate these problems. Do not neglect these effects of wounding. They may frustrate the overall aim of good management - a return of the individual to as near normal function as possible.

Lymphatics 141

146

The Hospital Environment

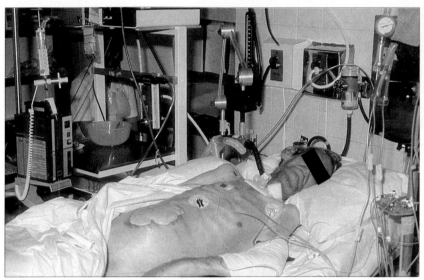

The intensive therapy unit

Which wounds and why?

The size or complicating features of a wound will influence where it is treated. Major or complicated wounds require the constantly available treatment and facilities of a hospital.

A hospital is a highly technical, labour intensive and costly environment staffed by teams of specialists. All domestic needs are met and behaviour can be supervised. In the intensive therapy unit, all decisions concerning the patient's life are taken by medical and nursing staff.

For instance, a patient with a large burn will require specialist medical and nursing care, physiotherapy, occupational therapy, the expertise of a dietitian, and probably a nutritionist, bacteriologist, pharmacist, orthotist and many others. Operating theatres, lung ventilation equipment, pressure relieving beds and other facilities may also be required. All these will be available in the specialist unit.

Changing practice

The cause of the wound may also influence the place of treatment. Traumatic wounds, even very minor ones such as a pretibial laceration, may present at the hospital accident and emergency department, where patients will receive initial care. The majority of surgical wounds occur in the hospital environment. However, with the increase in day case surgery, earlier postoperative discharge and minor surgery by general practitioners, surgical wound care is now an important part of community practice. Many surgical wound complications may now present in the community, eg infection. In a recent prospective series of postoperative wound infection in general surgery, 5.9% occurred in hospital while 9.2% developed in the community.

Orthotist G

Community 148

147

Community Environments

Most patients with a wound will be treated at home. Some implications of this are examined.

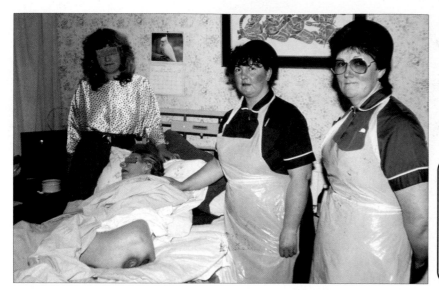

Patient and carers in the home environment.

Of all leg ulcer patients, 83% are managed in the community, 12% attend out-patient departments, only 1% are admitted to hospital.

Care in the community

The majority of wounds can be classified as moderate to minor. As such, they are suitable for treatment in the community. Delivery of care tends to be intermittent in this setting. Some facilities are available at health centres and nursing homes or are supplied to individual patients in their homes.

Dressings in the community

The first requirement of a dressing is that it should be effective in promoting healing. To be effective it must also be feasible. A management plan which is to be implemented in the community must take into account the intermittent nature of care, the limitations of the carer's time, the extent of disruption to the patient's life and how this may affect compliance. Ease of use of a dressing and the need for less frequent changes are important in this setting. For instance, although compression bandaging of the leg speeds venous ulcer healing, it creates difficulties for the patient with footwear, mobility, bathing and the need for frequent reapplication by a professional.

Problems may arise when a patient is discharged from hospital. Both the district nurse and the general practitioner should be informed, to ensure continuity of care. A three day supply of dressings from the hospital will allow time for the nurse to obtain a prescription from the patient's general practitioner.

Home modifications

Chronic wounds, or the long term consequences of healed wounds, e.g. amputation, may justify assistance for permanent alterations in the individual's situation. Rehousing or modifications to accommodation may be necessary to allow access to the house and toilet facilities.

Disruption

Compression 171

Chronic leg ulceration: socio-economic aspects. Lothian and Forth Valley leg ulcer study. Callum M J, Harper D R, Dale J, Ruckley C V. Scott Med J 1988; 33: 358-360.

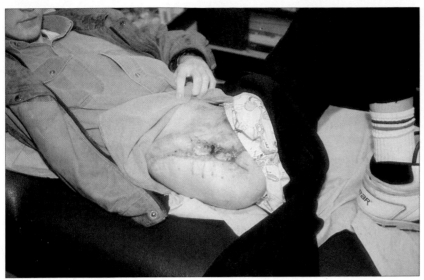

This patient dresses his wound himself

Stages of management

 Wound management requires

- assessment of patient and wound,
- formulation of a treatment plan,
- implementation of the plan,
- monitoring of progress.
- modification of the plan.

Individual or team care

 These functions may all be performed by one person or by several individuals. Their training and the continuity of care are the important parameters. In hospital, various health care professionals co-operate to provide care. Professionals in the community need a broad knowledge base and ingenuity in adapting to local conditions. The primary health care team is drawn from different professional backgrounds with various areas of expertise, eg health visitors, general practitioners, practice and district nurses. They also liaise with other professionals, such as social workers.

Self or lay carers

A patient or relative may administer first aid or provide uncomplicated wound care. This is convenient, available and economical. Such a lay carer needs practical and clear guidelines on when to seek help. Regular monitoring by a professional is still required. For example, the parent of a scalded toddler should immediately remove the child's clothes and apply cool water while obtaining medical help. Following discharge from hospital, simple dressing of the burn may be carried out by the parent.

Hospital 147

Support Facilities

Some members of the support team

Where to treat

The patient, as well as the wound, should to be considered when deciding where to supply treatment. The wound adds an extra burden to a patient's situation which may result in the need for additional support. The form of support will depend on the degree and nature of care required. If the patient is in the community, this may take the form of help with shopping for a housebound patient or temporary admission to an institution.

Range of resources

A wide range of resources and personnel is available to support patients in the community. Health visitors, domestic carers and lay sitters assist patients in their homes. The voluntary sector is also active with schemes such as Crossroads, Meals on Wheels, Gingerbread and various self-help groups offering support. Facilities like a day centre may allow older patients to remain at home. Family centres can help parents to cope better with their children. Different types of institutional care are also available. Simple supervision for the elderly in sheltered housing, domestic care in a residential home, domestic and nursing care in a nursing home are examples. Respite care may be arranged in hospital to allow family carers a holiday or if the carer is unwell. Financial support may be available for individuals who give up work to care for a relative.

Specialist services

Some wound types have specialised needs during healing and once healed. Permanent disabilities (eg amputations) may necessitate the provision of supports or prostheses, and training in their use. Surgical procedures which create a stoma have a marked practical and psychological impact on the patient's life. A stoma therapist can be an invaluable source of information and reassurance.

Crossroads G
Gingerbread G

150

Section 7
The Health Care System

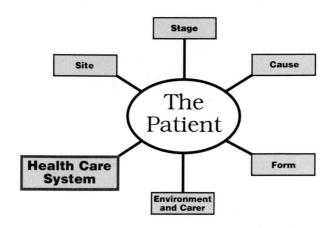

The Wound Organiser

The facilities available to you to manage wounds ultimately depend on the resources available in your particular health care system. The final factor of the Organiser explores this relationship.

Different types of health care system are explained in this section.

Guide to Section 7

Health Care Systems

Type of system	Funding	Effect
Private (uninsured)	Care provided according to individual's purchasing power.	The best care for those who can afford to pay. No provision for the poor.
Private insurance	Care provided according to benefits purchased and rules of company.	The best care for those accepted for insurance. No provision for the uninsured.
State insurance	Care provided by private sector. Insurance funded by state.	Care for all members of society. Level of funding and care a political issue.
State system	Care provided by state. Funded by state from taxation.	Care for all members of society. Level of funding and care a political issue.
Charitable organisations	Care provided according to donations and rules of charity.	Care for specified groups, conditions or places.

Financing Health Care

Affluence can influence the type or sophistication of treatment in some countries.

Sources of funds

 Health care systems provide care for illness and disability. One of the definitive characteristics of these systems is their funding.

- Privately funded by the individual requiring care,
- Private or state insurance schemes,
- State funded through general taxation,
- Charitable organisations.

North America

 In the USA, the provision of health care is largely a commercial undertaking, and most citizens insure against health expenditure. State and federal government have had to introduce schemes (Medicaid, Medicare) to help the poor and elderly, who might otherwise be denied care. In Canada, the state pays an insurance premium for every individual. All citizens are thus insured by the state and care is provided by independent, private institutions and health care professionals.

USA

The United Kingdom

 The United Kingdom's National Health Service is funded from general taxation. Health care is provided free of charge at the point of delivery to all citizens according to their need. Any individual, however, may choose to purchase health care from private suppliers, either from personal funds or via an insurance scheme.

Developing countries

 In most of the developing world, resources are scarce and the need great. State health care resources are supplemented by international aid agencies and charitable organisations.

Do you think the type of health care system can affect the patient/doctor relationship?

America's uninsured and underinsured. Judge K. Br Med J 1991; **302**: 1163.
International health care expenditure trends. Schieber G, Poullier J P. Health Affairs 1989; **8**: 169-177.

Control and Distribution of Services

Limited resources

 As medical science has developed, more sophisticated treatments have become available - many of which are very costly. An aging population in many western countries has led to increasing demands for health care. State resources are finite and governments must find ways of limiting expenditure.

UK regulations

An example in the UK is the Drug Tariff. This limits the availability, on an NHS prescription, of some drugs and dressings in the community. Some materials provided in hospitals are not available in the community.

Another practical point is that a standard charge is made for each item, not the quantity, on a prescription. Although children, pensioners and those with specified chronic conditions can claim exemption, others can not. It is important that a generous quantity is prescribed to avoid an unnecessary financial penalty. In reality, only about 15% of patients do pay the full prescription charge.

Drug Tariff

The Drug Tariff. Department of Health. London: HMSO, 1990.

The outcome movement - will it get us where we want to go? Epstein A M. N Eng J Med 1990; **323**: 266-269.

Priorities in Health Care

There are also differences in the priorities applied to the provision of health care.

Geographical differences

 In industrialised countries most infectious diseases have been controlled and resources are concentrated on the diseases associated with an affluent society. Prevention of these conditions is receiving more emphasis and money is available for public health education programmes.

In the developing countries, inadequate nutrition, poor hygiene and infectious disease have yet to be overcome. Resources are often insufficient to provide even basic care to the whole population. Public health measures, such as clean water and vaccination programmes, are a priority.

Nutrition 106

Government established priorities

 In the UK, a higher priority is now given to community, as opposed to hospital based, care. For this to work, resources are necessary for the provision of community support. This involves social services and the welfare system, as well as health care services. Day centres, family centres, grants to adapt homes or provision for rehousing, carer's allowance, and mobility allowances can improve an individual's ability to cope in the community.

Priority
Community 148
Hospital 147

Should tattoos be removed under the NHS?

Rationing: at the cutting edge. Cochrane M, Hain G. Br Med J 1991; **303**: 1039-1042.

Developing principles for prudent health care allocation: the continuing Oregon experiment. Crawshaw R. West J. Med 1990; **152**: 441-446.

155

Guide to Section 8

Now that you know how to use the Organiser you are in a position to formulate appropriate treatment plans.

Read this section for guidelines for treating wounds

Wound Dressings

Use the Wound Organiser to assess the patient's needs. Then use this simplified chart to help you select a dressing with the required features.

Dressing Feature	Multi-layer Gauze	Paraffin Gauze	Poly-urethane films	Alginates	Hydro-gels	Hydro-colloids
Moisture retention			✓	Plus secondary ✓ dressing	Plus secondary ✓ dressing	✓
Absorption	✓			✓	✓	✓
Debridement by autolysis			✓	✓	✓	✓
Non adherent to wound			✓	✓	✓	✓
Self-retaining			✓			✓
Delivery of medication		✓			✓	
Dressing reduces pain			✓	✓	✓	✓
Support			✓			✓
Low unit cost	✓	✓				
Cost effectiveness			✓	✓	✓	✓
Secondary dressing not required			✓			✓

Tools for Wound Healing

Management of a patient with a wound may involve several different approaches.

Our tools for the treatment of wounds are all too often used incorrectly or for the wrong reason.

Assessment of priorities

The dramatic appearance of a traumatic wound may cause it to become the focus of attention. Resuscitative measures - airway maintenance, controlling haemorrhage and supporting circulation - must be given priority. A general assessment must be carried out, to detect less obvious, but life threatening, conditions such as head injuries.

Formulation of treatment plan

Good wound management requires accurate assessment of all the Organiser factors, so that the best possible conditions for healing can be provided. A good treatment plan includes factors relating to the patient's general condition, environment and behaviour as well as to the wound. Wound treatment may include cleansing, debriding, dressing, surgery or systemic measures. Close monitoring of progress is essential and modification of treatment may be required at any stage.

Patient education

The information given to the patient is an important part of the treatment plan. For instance, factors which may lead to recurrence of a foot ulcer should be explained to a diabetic patient. Advice includes regular washing and adequate drying with a soft towel. Wearing footwear while ambulant is essential. Comfortable footwear, non-synthetic socks or stockings and frequent help from the chiropodist are vital. The patient should also be encouraged to seek help quickly for even the most minor foot problems. A decision on whether the patient is to be managed at home or in hospital depends on the severity of the problem, the patient's social support, and the availability of treatment in the community. Foot complications are the commonest cause of hospital admission for diabetics.

Cleansing 160
Debriding 161
and 168

Diabetic 128

Wound Cleansing

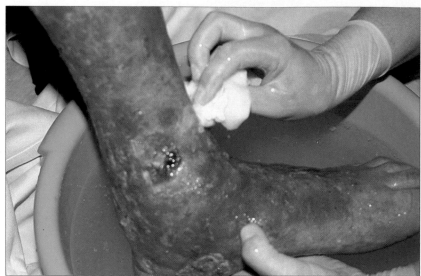
The wound should be gently cleansed.

"First, do no harm."
Hippocrates

The need for cleansing	Wounds likely to be contaminated require thorough cleansing, to remove loose debris, foreign material and bacteria. Cleansing should not cause further damage to viable or healing tissues.	**Contaminated 114**
Cleansing methods	Copious irrigation with normal saline or a non-ionic fluid is recommended as the gentlest method. In the past, a number of strong solutions, such as hydrogen peroxide, were used for cleansing. They have not been shown to benefit the wound and there is in vitro evidence that they damage living cells. A chronic wound or any cavity wound may be cleansed by soaking in a bath or shower. Adherent dressings are more easily removed by soaking. However it should be remembered that not all patients have ready access to such facilities at home. Some cultures and religions prohibit bathing in non-running water or removal of body hair. After initial cleansing the wound should be closely inspected. A soft scrubbing brush may be needed to remove fine particles of foreign material. Exploration in theatre may be indicated for deeper wounds. Anaesthesia, either local or general may be required for adequate cleansing.	**Non-ionic G**
Tattooing	Foreign material left in a superficial wound can become incorporated in the healing surface. This results in an unsightly traumatic tattoo. Dermabrasion or excision are then necessary to remove this.	**Dermabrasion G**

A child presents to you on Bonfire Night with an abrasion on his cheek which is heavily contaminated with wood ash. What is the likely appearance of the wound one year later if you fail to clean it thoroughly?

Surgical Wound Debridement

Debridement will be necessary in certain situations.

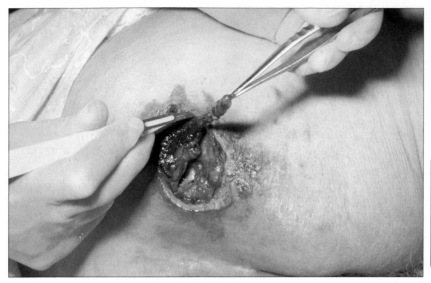

Surgical debridement.

The quickest way to remove dead tissue is to excise it.

Removal of dead tissue

Debridement is defined as the removal from a wound of dead or damaged tissue. The presence of such tissue within the wound delays healing, and predisposes to infection. Debridement is therefore an essential step to promote healing. It may be carried out surgically or by the action of dressings. The need for debridement is indicated by the history of the injury or the clinical appearance of the wound.

Examples of surgical debridement

Surgical debridement of a fresh traumatic wound may be a simple matter of trimming irregular wound edges. In severe wounds, removal of any dead or damaged muscle and tendon is essential. Small amounts of dead tissue can be carefully excised from chronic wounds at routine dressing changes. This should be a painless procedure. In those with impaired sensation, care is required not to damage viable but insensate tissue. Excessive necrotic material in a chronic wound may be excised surgically to speed healing.

Anti-tetanus regime

Traumatic wounds, especially those associated with soil contamination, run the risk of inoculation with tetanus spores. These can germinate and multiply in anaerobic conditions (eg devitalised deep tissue). Clostridium tetani releases potent toxins which affect the neuromuscular system, producing widespread muscular spasm. Immunisation programmes greatly reduced the incidence of tetanus. When a non-immunised individual sustains a deep, contaminated wound, consider administering tetanus immunoglobulin as well as a course of tetanus toxoid to induce immunisation. The immunoglobulin and toxoid should be administered at different sites. Repeat administration of tetanus toxoid within five years is not recommended. Prophylactic penicillin is also required.

Tetanus. In: Immunization against infectious disease. DHSS. London: HMSO, 1988a; 25-29.

Delay 103

Dressings 168

Tetanus

Clostridium G

161

Wound Closure

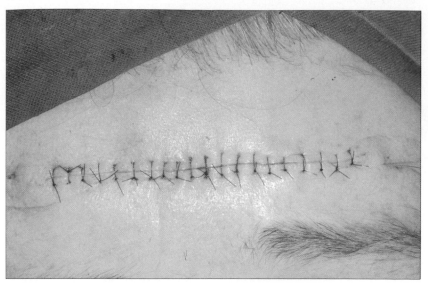

Surgical wound closed with sutures

Why close a wound?

Closure of a wound reduces the tissue proliferation required and the scar tissue formed. An intact surface is more quickly reconstructed, lessening the risks associated with an open wound and leaving a linear scar.

Where tissue has been lost, the defect may be too great for the wound edges to be apposed. Surgical methods - such as split or full thickness skin grafting, skin flaps, or composite flaps - can be used to fill the defect. These can speed healing, produce a more cosmetically acceptable result and protect exposed structures.

Wound edges may be brought together by

- sutures,
- wound closure strips,
- clips.

Sutures

Sutures (stitches) are made from a variety of materials with different characteristics, eg strength, tissue reaction, absorption rates. They can be divided broadly into absorbable and non-absorbable, examples of the latter being silk, nylon and prolene. Absorbable sutures have ranges of absorption rate.

- Catgut, variable but usually within three weeks;
- Polyglactin, 6 to 14 weeks;
- Polyglycolic, 10 days to 4 months;
- Polydioxamine, 3 to 6 months.

Metal clips appose the skin edges externally. They are quick and easy to apply and remove but are relatively expensive.

The choice of wound closure method will depend on the nature of the wound and the perceived risk of wound complications. Contaminated wounds, with high risk of infection, require non-absorbable sutures, such as nylon or prolene. Clean wounds can be closed by absorbable sutures, as there is a low risk of infection. Curved needles are frequently used for suturing - wound edges can be more easily everted and there is a lower risk of needle puncture to the operator. Wound closure strips can be used for minor wounds. They avoid the need for sutures, with their associated trauma, in wounds requiring less apposition force.

Sutures - properties of individual suture materials. Eden C G. Surgery, Oxford Add-on-Series. 1991; **95**: 2271a.

Sutures
Wound closure
strip G

Contaminated 114

Dressings

Physical forms of dressings
SHEET
GEL
COLLOID
FILM
WEAVE
FOAM

Functions

Dressings have a number of functions. They may
- protect the wound and retain moisture,
- absorb exudate blood and odour,
- debride the wound,
- provide a contact surface,
- influence perceived pain,
- support the wound.

Dressing materials are now available in a wide range of physical forms and with differing properties. It is important to have some idea of the strengths and weaknesses of the different types of dressings. A dressing may perform one or more of the functions listed above.

Choosing a dressing

Before choosing a dressing, first determine what the wound requires to promote healing. A full assessment, using the Wound Organiser, should provide this information. The list of wound requirements, eg promotion of granulation, debridement, promotion of epithelialisation, can then be compared with the properties of the various dressing materials available. If a number of dressings satisfy the wound's needs, the final choice is made by considering relative efficacy, cost, convenience, patient acceptability and unwanted effects.

Cost implications

The best use of resources requires that all aspects of treatment are considered together. Like should only be compared with like. For instance, although some of the modern dressing materials appear more expensive than simple traditional forms, this may be offset by the savings - in less frequent changes, less nursing time used or speedier healing. At present, the cost of nursing time is the largest element in total cost of treating conditions such as leg ulcers.

Which dressing and why? Turner T D. In: Wound Care. Westaby S. (ed). London: Heinemann, 1985; 59-69.

163

Dressings: Protective Barrier Properties

In this page we provide an update on the barrier properties of dressings in current use.

Physical barrier

 Dressings have been used for centuries to protect the wound from the external environment. The dressing forms a physical barrier, which may exclude external agents, retain moisture and exudate factors, and reduce heat loss by insulating the wound. All these actions help to create a favourable local environment in the wound. All dressing materials have some protective barrier properties, but modern synthetic dressings give effective protection in a wide range of situations.

Range of protection

 Simple dressings are often used for sutured wounds, where the benefits of non-adherence and hydration are less obvious, though still applicable. Transparent film dressings of polyurethane or polyethylene are permeable to water vapour, oxygen and other gases but not to water or bacteria. These dressings are commonly used to isolate an area, eg first stage pressure sore, from maceration and friction. Hydrocolloid sheets are layered dressings, impermeable to water and bacteria, which insulate the wound from heat losses. Some hydrocolloids are also impermeable to oxygen and so help create a hypoxic wound environment, which encourages angiogenesis.

Convenience

 Modern synthetic dressings are convenient. They may

- isolate the wound, allowing the patient to bath or shower;
- protect from contamination, e.g. urine, faeces;
- be flexible, allowing an earlier return to normal function;
- be easy to apply;
- be designed to remain in place for longer periods.

Infection

 The introduction of opaque hydrocolloid sheet dressings, designed to be left undisturbed for several days, raised concern about the development of infection beneath the dressing. A study in 1978 showed an overgrowth of commensal skin bacteria under occlusive conditions. Subsequent clinical trials, using oxygen impermeable hydrocolloids in the treatment of leg ulcers, have not shown an increase in infection rates.

Sore 126

Angiogenesis 98

Commensal 104

164

Dressings: Moisture Retention

Here we discuss a protective function of modern dressings crucial for improved healing: maintenance of a moist environment.

Crusted wound.

The effect of drying

In undamaged skin, the cells of the dermis and the deeper layers of the epidermis are bathed in tissue fluid. Damage to the outer layers of the skin allows the tissues to dry out and a zone of additional cell death results from desiccation. An exposed wound will tend to form a scab, or crust, of cellular debris and protein.

Effects of occlusion

An occlusive covering to the wound maintains a moist atmosphere and prevents the formation of crust. The polyurethane films and composite hydrocolloid sheet dressings seal the wound and retain wound exudate. Hydrocolloids and alginates act with the exudate to form a moist gel over the wound surface. The alginates and some of the hydrogel preparations gradually lose moisture by evaporation. Unless given an impermeable covering, they will slowly allow the wound to dry particularly where exudate is light.

Moisture and epithelialisation

In 1962, Winter showed that crusted wounds epithelialised more slowly than covered wounds. Epithelialisation involves cell migration. Enzymes, such as collagenases and proteinases, apparently enable cells to migrate across the wound in moist areas where fibrin is deposited. When a wound has been allowed to dry and crust has formed, the epithelial cells must penetrate to a deeper level to find a suitably moist plane. Additional time and metabolic activity are thus required to heal a crusted wound.

Formation of the scab and the rate of epithelialisation of superficial wounds in the skin of the young domestic pig. Winter G D. Nature 1962; **193**: 293-294.

The effect of occlusive dressings on collagen synthesis in superficial wounds. Alvarez O M, Mertz P M and Eaglestein W H. J Surg Res 1983; **35**: 142-148.

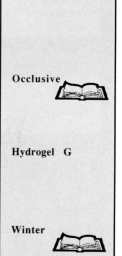

Occlusive

Hydrogel G

Winter

Dressings: Absorption

Dressings function in the control of symptoms. Here we explain the absorptive role of various types of dressings.

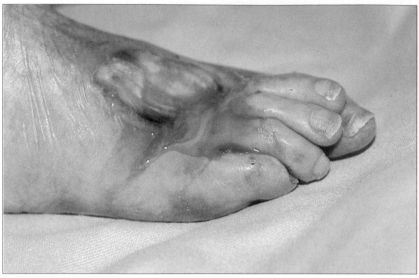

Wound with marked exudate.

Traditional dressings

Modern dressings

 Gauze and cotton wool have been used as dressing materials for centuries. The woven nature of gauze facilitates absorption. It acts like a wick, drawing fluid away from the wound. Pads of cotton wool or Gamgee are light and airy, allowing moisture to evaporate, keeping the outer parts of the dressing dry and inhibiting the entry of bacteria.

 Polyurethane films allow the evaporation of water vapour, but this is limited by their transpiration rate. Thus fluid may accumulate under the film. Alginates, hydrocolloids and hydrogel contain hydrophilic polymers with absorptive properties. Leakage or soak-through of exudate occurs when the volume of exudate exceeds the dressing's absorptive or transpiratory properties. These properties vary with different dressings. Leakage from under a composite hydrocolloid sheet indicates a breach in the bacterial barrier but, in practice, infection rates do not appear to be increased. A sudden leakage from an occlusive dressing may distress and worry the patient even if it is not detrimental to the wound. The dressing should be changed and the patient reassured.

The amount of exudate from a wound and the frequency with which the carer can change the dressing will have a bearing on the choice of dressing, especially in the community.

Gamgee G

Transpiration rate G

Exudate 95

Community 148

Dressings: Odour

Dressings are one of the ways the effect of a foul smelling wound can be diminished.

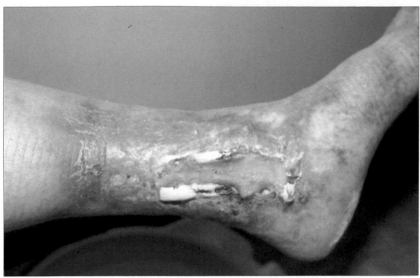

The presence of pseudomonas imparts a greenish colour to dressings.

Sniffing a dressing may not seem "high tech" but it can alert you to infection.

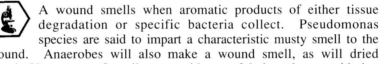

Foul smelling wounds

A wound smells when aromatic products of either tissue degradation or specific bacteria collect. Pseudomonas species are said to impart a characteristic musty smell to the wound. Anaerobes will also make a wound smell, as will dried blood. Your sense of smell can provide a useful clue when considering presence and causes of wound infection.

Management of offensive wounds

Fungating tumours may present considerable management problems. The convoluted nature of the wound makes cleaning difficult. Exudate may be profuse in quantity and foul smelling. Smell can be ameliorated by frequent irrigation and fresh dressings, the use of absorbent charcoal dressings, and deodorant powders or solutions. Metronidazole rectally, by mouth, as a gauze soak or mixed with a hydrogel reduces anaerobic bacteria in the wound and is reported to minimise odour. Plain live yogurt is used as a dressing, to alter the bacteriological balance of the wound. Lactobacilli supervene, decreasing the numbers of other organisms and thus reducing smell.

Effects of smell

A foul smelling wound has marked social implications. The aware patient is embarrassed and inhibited by it. Relatives and friends can be nauseated by the smell, and may be less able to offer their support. This is particularly relevant with some advanced carcinomas. Deodorant impregnated tags and air cleaning machines will maintain an acceptable atmosphere in the patient's room.

Patients with abdominal stomas may worry about leakage, smell and social embarrassment. The provision of information, referral to a stoma therapist and contact with the appropriate self-help group, eg Ileostomy Association, will help them cope with these and other concerns.

Pseudomonas 104

Metronidazole 167

167

Dressings: Debridement

We have discussed surgical debridement. Now we look at the use of dressings to debride.

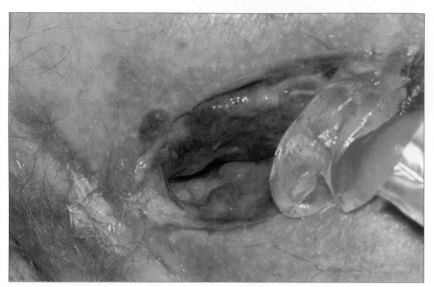

Hydrogel in use for a cavity wound.

Modes of action

Dressings may debride in the following ways

- mechanically,
- chemically,
- enzymatically,
- through promotion of autolysis.

Traditionally, the alternate application of wet (saline) and dry gauze was used to assist debridement. The gauze adhered to the unwanted material and gradually lifted it, piecemeal, out of the wound. This was effective but labour intensive, caused discomfort and disrupted the wound.

Chemical agents such as malic acid, alone or mixed with benzoic and salicylic acids, and enzymes (eg streptokinase and streptodornase) are available as wound dressings. These are designed to render necrotic material more soluble. Because they are relatively caustic, their use should be limited. Care must be taken not to damage the surrounding intact skin, especially when dealing with chronic wounds.

Modern synthetic dressings, eg hydrocolloids, hydrogels and films, provide a moist wound environment and promote sloughing of necrotic tissue by autolysis.

Current controversy

Hypochlorite soaks, eg Eusol, have been used in dirty wounds since about 1915. They are an effective antiseptic. Recent studies have demonstrated an in vitro cytotoxic effect with adverse vascular and cellular changes in clean wounds. Hypochlorites are not indicated for clean, granulating wounds. How the in vitro evidence and studies of clean wounds apply to dirty or infected wounds remains to be elucidated. The use of hypochlorite soaks in dirty wounds remains contentious. The adverse effects of hypochlorites should be weighed against the known cytotoxic effects of infecting organisms.

Eusol - to use or not to use? Cunliffe W J. Dermatology in Practice April/May 1990: 5-7.

Hypochlorite G

Dressings: Adhesion and Delivery

Here we explore the effects of contact between the dressing and the wound surface.

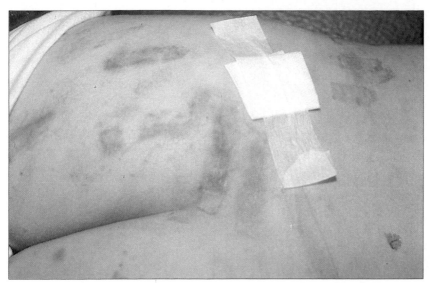

Allergic reaction to adhesive tape used to secure dressings.

Effects of adhesion

Wound dressings are in close contact with the healing surface. Adhesion to the wound and possible incorporation of the dressing can occur, leading to pain, disruption and bleeding when a dressing is changed. However, a dressing which adheres to the surrounding, intact skin has certain advantages and is convenient for patient and carer. It seals the wound and avoids the use of adhesive tape. However, disruption of newly formed epithelium is a risk if care is not exercised during dressing removal.

Prevention

Dry gauze will adhere to a raw wound surface and, if left, will become embedded in the granulation tissue. A number of materials have been developed to act as a non-adherent intervening layer. These include material meshes impregnated with paraffin, woven viscose or nylon and plastic films. All these are only partially non-adherent. Hydrocolloids, gels, films and alginates do not adhere to the moist wound surface. Hydrocolloid and film dressings do adhere to dry skin. Care is therefore required in removal, particularly in patients with fragile skin or where new epidermis has formed. These dressings are designed to be changed less frequently, which will help to minimise this problem.

Medicated dressings

The contact layer of the dressing may be used to deliver antiseptics or antibiotics. These may be incorporated into paraffin gauze type dressings or hydrogels. The major problem with any topical application is the potential for induction of allergic sensitivity reactions. Because topical antibiotics may also lead to the development of resistant strains of bacteria, they are generally restricted in use. Topical administration is generally limited to those unsuitable for systemic use, e.g. framycetin.

Contact sensitivity in community-based leg ulcer patients. Kulozik M, Powell S M, Cherry G and Ryan T J. Clin Exp Dermatol 1988; **13**: 82-84.

Pain 170

Granulation 99

Sensitivity

Dressings: Pain

Here we look at wound pain - its causes and implications.

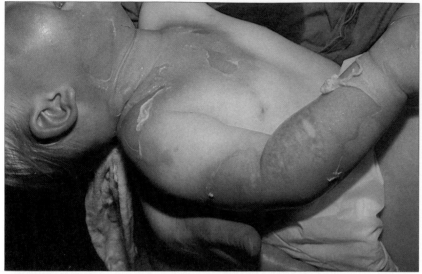

Painful dressing changes - time to reconsider dressing material choice and if repeat dressings are needed.

Increased frequency of dressings increases the demand on resources.

Causes of pain

 Pain results from the brain's interpretation of neural messages generated at the wound site by stimulation of nerve endings. This may be caused by

- inflammation,
- movement of, or pressure on, local tissues,
- shearing of the dressing over the wound surface,
- removal of the dressing,
- irritant cleansing substances,
- exposure to the atmosphere,
- wound complications.

These physical factors are exacerbated by emotions, eg fear or anxiety.

Implications of pain

Some discomfort is associated with most wounds, but increasing or continued pain should be seen as a warning. The wound should immediately be inspected, a cause for the pain sought and appropriate action taken. Pain may be due to increasing tissue tension or pressure (eg wound haematoma or too tight a dressing) which can result in tissue necrosis. Pain is also a symptom of wound infection.

Dressings and pain

From the patient's point of view, one of the major criteria for judging a dressing is the degree of associated pain. Recently developed dressings, which form a gel over the wound surface, are less painful while in place. They may also be easier and less painful to remove. Their design allows less frequent changes than traditional dressings, although this may require the expertise of a health care professional. A full explanation prior to any procedure has been shown to reduce anxiety and the degree of pain experienced. Nevertheless, some dressing changes will require analgesia. A range of analgesics - from IV opiates, inhalation of nitrous oxide, non-steroidal anti-inflammatory drugs, to simple paracetamol - may be employed, depending on the severity of the pain.

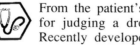 *Pain mechanisms: a new theory.* Melzack R and Wall P D. Int Science 1965; **150**: 971-997.

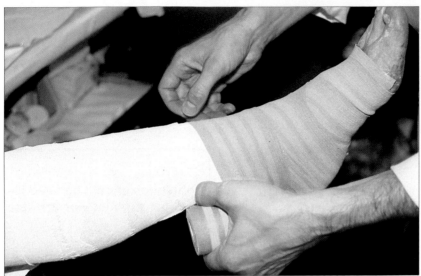

Multiple bandage layers for adequate compression.

Functions

The outer layers of the dressing are important for a number of reasons. They may support the wound and surrounding tissues, maintain the position of contact layers, absorb moisture, control oedema, or act as a splint. There are numerous ways of holding dressings in place. The dressing materials themselves may be adhesive. Adhesive tapes of various types are available. The dressing may be secured with sutures, held in place with "garments" of elasticated net or by a wide range of bandages.

Bandages

The ability of a bandage to retain a dressing, and support or compress the wound, is largely determined by its elastic properties. Pressures beneath the bandage are a function of the tension of application, width of bandage and the radius of the limb. It is important to be aware of the hazards of inappropriate or excessive use of pressure. For example, in arterial ulcers where perfusion pressures are low, it is important not to apply compression - complete capillary bed collapse may occur, leading to anoxia and further tissue damage.

External pressure

In treating venous ulceration, an applied external pressure gradient from ankle to knee is advocated. This counteracts the raised capillary pressures consequent on venous hypertension. Oedema fluid is transferred back into the vascular or lymphatic channels. Venous velocity is increased and venous pooling reduced. Recommended pressure levels may vary from 18-24 mm Hg to 40-50 mm Hg. Failure to appreciate the value of compression may lead to inappropriate selection of bandages or inadequate application. Even when using self-adherent dressing materials, bandaging may still be necessary to exert pressure.

Hazards
Arterial 124

Venous   123

Lymphatic 141
Pressure 87

Hazards of compression treatment of the leg: an estimate from Scottish surgeons. Callum M J, Ruckley C V, Dale J J and Harper D R. Br Med J 1987; **295**: 1382.

Systemic Measures: Antibiotics

Here we explain how antibiotics may be used in wound management.

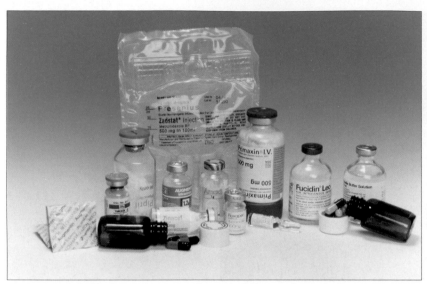

Antibiotics come in a number of different formulations.

Antibiotics should be used like a sniper's bullet not an atom bomb.

Actions

Antibiotics may be bacteriostatic, preventing multiplication, or bactericidal, resulting in the death of the organisms. Bacteria display sensitivity or resistance to the effects of individual antibiotics or families of antibiotics.

Mode of use

Antibiotics are used either to treat an established infection (eg cellulitis, septicaemia) or prophylactically, to prevent infection. If the causative organism has been isolated, its susceptibility to various antibiotics can be determined by the laboratory and the appropriate drug administered. When the organism has not yet been identified or when antibiotics are used prophylactically, the choice of antibiotic is made on the probabilities of particular organisms being causative. When used prophylactically, only a short course of three to four doses is prescribed. Broad spectrum antibiotics or a combination of drugs are used. Antibiotics may be administered by mouth, or parenterally. Topical use is rarely indicated in wound care.

The target organisms

Bacteria vary in their ability to produce infection. Those associated with disease are termed pathogenic. Organisms commonly causing skin infection include Staphylococci, Streptococci, Clostrida, Pseudomonas, E coli, Klebsiellae and anaerobic organisms such as Bacteroides.

Cellulitis 94
Septicaemia 105

Topical 169

Clostrida 161

172

Other Systemic or Alternative Measures

A wide range of other measures may be employed to promote a successful outcome for particular wounds.

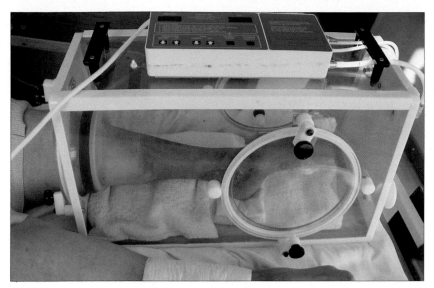

Application of hyperbaric oxygen to leg

General measures

The treatment of a patient with a wound includes measures to improve general health, such as dietary advice and nutritional support, adequate analgesia, anti-depressants and relaxation techniques. In many circumstances, eg a hand injury, the outcome of treatment can be greatly influenced by the patient's motivation. Hence a positive state of mind and good understanding of how treatment will help should be encouraged.

Physical modes of treatment

A number of physical forms of wound treatment are known. Microampage electric currents have been shown to promote healing of dermal wounds, when the anode is applied to the wound. The effects of treatment with ultrasound, low powered He-Ne laser and ultraviolet have all been investigated, but are not yet established treatments.

Hyperbaric oxygen

Hyperbaric oxygen is said to increase the level of oxygen in the tissues of the wound, to reduce oedema and to retard bacterial growth.

Local

Local application of hyperbaric oxygen, at various pressure levels and for various treatment times, has been employed for a wide range of chronic wounds and positive results reported. Further controlled trials are needed to define the indications for, and parameters of, treatment.

Systemic

Similarly, systemic treatment in a hyperbaric chamber is said to give improved healing, especially in ischaemic wounds. This also needs further study. The value of systemic treatment for gas gangrene infections is well established. Treatment increases the oxygen tension in the tissue, which inhibits the growth of the anaerobic infective organisms.

173

The Wound Programme

An explanation of terminology

174

Glossary

Abscess — A localised collection of pus in a cavity formed by disintegration of tissue. — 113, 120, 128, 137

Albumin — A soluble protein, a major component of serum proteins and largely responsible for osmotic pressure. — 106

Alginates — Wound dressing products derived from seaweed. Absorbent, haemostatic dressings of calcium alginate, or calcium and sodium alginate, form a viscous gel over the wound surface. — 138, 165, 169

Angiogenesis — The process by which new blood vessels are formed. It occurs during the proliferative phase of wound healing and is stimulated by angiogenic growth factor. — 98, 99, 103, 107

Antibiotic — A compound which kills or prevents growth of micro-organisms. — 120, 128, 141, 169, 172

Antibody — Protein, produced by activated lymphocytes, which combines with foreign material, facilitating its removal. — 97

Arachidonic — A polyunsaturated fatty acid, precursor of prostacyclin, thromboxane A2, and leukotrienes. — 130, 180

Atherosclerosis — The hardening of blood vessels. A fatty deposit in the walls of large and medium sized arteries leads to a narrowing of the lumen, reducing blood flow. — 124, 128

Autolysis — The natural degradation of devitalised tissue. — 96, 140, 168

Bacteraemia — The presence of bacteria in the blood stream. — 105, 141

Callus — New tissue generated at the site of a fracture during bone healing. It is later replaced by hard, adult bone. — 75

Catabolic state — A destructive metabolic state during which complex molecules are broken down into simpler components. — 106

Cavitation — A phenomenon seen in gunshot wounds. A temporary cavity is induced in soft tissue, following the absorption of kinetic energy when a missile enters the tissues. — 114

Cellulitis — Inflammation of cellular tissue. Clinical picture associated with infection in the skin. Characterised by redness, heat, oedema, and pain. — 94, 172

Chemical mediators	Chemical substances which influence the activity of cells, acting as local messengers.	**86, 92, 93, 94, 95, 99**
Chemotaxis	The process involved when specific cellular activity occurs as a response to substances released into the tissues. For example, the migration of leucocytes to the wound site in response to a chemical concentration gradient.	**92, 95, 98**
Claudication (intermittent)	Pain due to ischaemia in the calf muscles, induced by muscle contractions. Typically, pain occurs on walking, increases until further exercise is impossible and is relieved by rest. Result of occlusive arterial diseases.	**124**
Clostridium	Genus of gram positive, spore forming bacteria.	**161**
Clot	A semi-solid mass formed from blood by a series of complex reactions.	**92, 136**
Collagen	The supportive, fibrous protein of skin, tendon, bone, cartilage and other connective tissue. Produced during the proliferative phase of healing and remodelled during maturation phase of healing.	**84, 92, 98, 99, 100, 101, 102, 107, 165**
Colonisation	The presence of bacteria on the surface of a wound.	**104**
Complement	A series of enzymatic proteins in the serum, concerned with immunological response and inflammation.	**94, 95**
Connective tissues	Mesodermal derived tissues which bind or support the structures of the body.	**100**
Contamination	The presence of foreign material (eg clothing, dirt) on or in a wound.	**125, 164**
Contact inhibition	A complex switching mechanism that turns off migration and mitosis when cells come in contact.	**100**
Contraction	Process occurring in a granulating wound by which the size of the raw area is reduced.	**98, 101, 111**
Contracture	Process occurring in maturing scar tissue by which the scar is shortened.	**98, 101**
Crohn's disease	Chronic inflammatory condition of the bowel, also called regional ileitis.	**137**

176

Crossroads	Organisation to provide lay carers in the community.	150
Cytokine	Substance produced by a cell as a local messenger to other cells.	92, 93
Debridement	Removal of dead tissue or foreign bodies from a wound.	96, 114, 119, 161, 163, 168
Deep vein thrombosis	Blood clot forming in the deep venous system of the legs.	122
Dehiscence	The breakdown of a closed wound, converting it to an open wound.	105, 109, 113
Dermabrasion	A surgical technique which removes the superficial layers of the skin.	160
Desiccation	The process of drying out.	81, 96, 100, 165
Diabetes mellitus	A disorder resulting from a fault in sugar metabolism. There is either a deficiency of the pancreatic hormone, insulin, or a lack of tissue sensitivity to its effects.	94, 121, 128
Doppler	Technique using ultrasound to detect blood flow in peripheral arteries. It is used to measure pressure within the arteries of the legs. Derived pressure ratios give an indication of the distal tissues' blood supply.	124
Elastin	The flexible, fibrous protein of elastic connective tissues.	84
Endothelium	Cellular lining of blood vessels.	92, 117, 136
Epithelialisation	Process by which the wound surface is covered by new epithelium.	95, 98, 100, 103, 107, 126, 136, 163, 165
Eschar	Dry, dead tissue adhering to a wound.	140
Escharotomy	Procedure during which the necrotic tissue (eschar) over the wound surface is divided.	118
Exudate	The fluid formed at the wound surface as a result of leakage from small vessels into the wound. Rich in protein and cells.	95, 102, 138, 164, 166, 167
Fibrin	An insoluble elastic protein derived from fibrinogen by the action of thrombin. Involved in the production of a blood clot.	92, 94, 100, 123, 163, 164, 165

177

Fibrinogen	A soluble precursor protein found in plasma. Converted to fibrin by thrombin.	92, 123
Fibroblast	The cell which produces collagen in healing wounds. It may differentiate into a myofibroblast.	92, 97, 98, 99, 102
Fibronectin	An elongated glycoprotein, with an array of binding sites, synthesised by fibroblasts and epithelial cells. Helps form the temporary matrix, over which migrating epithelial cells move during skin healing when the basement membrane has been destroyed.	100
Flap	A portion of tissue, often skin, which is partially separated from its original site.	87, 103, 116, 138, 162
Gamgee	Traditional dressing, made of cotton wool with a gauze covering. Invented by J S Gamgee (1828-1886), English Surgeon.	166
Gangrene	Historical descriptive term for dead tissue. Superadded infection produces a state called "wet gangrene".	96, 120, 173
Gauze	Loosely woven cotton mesh material. Traditional outer dressing.	138, 166, 167, 168, 169
Gingerbread	Organisation of single parent families.	150
Granulation tissue	The red, moist and fragile connective tissue that fills in the wound during the proliferative phase of healing.	84, 98, 99, 111, 120, 128, 138, 169
Haematoma	A collection of blood in the tissues.	91, 103, 105, 113, 136, 140, 170
Haemostasis	Processes that lead to reduction of blood loss from the body.	92, 136
Histamine	An amine found in mast cells. A powerful vasodilator, involved in the initial stages of inflammation and allergic reactions.	94, 130
Hydrocolloid	A colloid system in which water is the dispersion medium.	96, 99, 138, 164, 165, 166, 167
Hydrogel	A gel that has water as its dispersion medium.	165, 166, 167, 169
Hyperbaric	Ambient pressure is raised above atmospheric pressure.	173

Hypertrophic	Enlarged due to increase in size of constituent cells.	101, 107
Hypochlorite	Diluted solution of hypochlorous acid salts usually sodium.	168
Hypoxia	Low oxygen concentrations in tissue.	103, 113, 124
Iatrogenic	Resulting from the actions of health care workers. Now used for adverse effects produced by treatment.	130, 137
Immune system	The body's natural defence mechanisms.	97, 105, 130, 131
Indolent	Causing little pain, slow growing.	
Infection	A clinical event caused by the invasion of viable tissue or body fluids by micro-organisms.	81, 85, 86, 91, 94, 96, 98, 100, 103, 104, 105, 113, 114, 119, 120, 123, 124, 128, 136, 137, 138, 140, 141, 147, 161, 162, 164, 166, 167, 170, 172, 173
Inflammation	Initial response to injury, generally lasting several days. The inflammatory phase consists of short lived vasoconstriction, followed by vasodilation, oedema formation and the migration of cells into the area.	93, 94, 95, 98, 99, 105, 115, 126, 130, 131, 141, 170
Intent (primary or secondary)	Manner of wound healing.	119, 136
Intima	The inner, endothelial, lining of blood vessels.	115
Ischaemia	Localised deficiency of blood, caused by functional constriction or actual obstruction of blood vessels.	87, 125, 126
Keloid	Scar tissue that progressively enlarges because of excess collagen formation. Keloids are red, raised, pruritic and tend to expand beyond the area of the original wound.	102
Keratin	Insoluble protein forming principal component of epidermis, hair, nails and tooth enamel.	81, 83
Keratinocyte	An epithelial cell. They form 95% of epidermal cells and synthesise keratin.	83, 97, 100

Laminin	A glycoprotein in the extracellular matrix which allows epithelial cells to attach to connective tissue.	**100**
Leprosy	A chronic, destructive disease caused by Mycobacterium leprae.	**86, 121**
Leukotriene	Derived from arachidonic acid. Acts as local hormone with short half life, being inactivated by many different tissues. Mediates allergic and inflammatory responses.	**94, 95**
Lobule	Subdivision of a lobe.	
Lymphocyte	A type of white blood cell, involved in the immune response.	**97, 141**
Lysosome	Body visible, under electron microscopy, in the cytoplasm of cells. Contains enzymes, mainly hydrolytic, which are released in response to cellular injury.	**96**
Macrophage	A cell derived from the blood monocyte. Phagocytic cell which plays a vital role in inflammation and initiates angiogenesis.	**92, 95, 96, 97, 99, 120**
Malignancy	Tumour with properties of anaplasia, invasion and metastasis.	**75, 129, 130, 137**
Marjolin	French physician (1780-1850) who described the occurrence of squamous cell carcinoma in old burn scars. Used to denote malignant change in scar or chronic wounds.	**129**
Mast cell	A cell derived from a basophil. Releases histamine during the inflammatory phase of healing.	
Matrix	Ground substance or framework.	**84, 98, 99, 100**
Maturation phase	The third and final stage of healing. May last months to years as the scar tissue is remodelled.	**93, 101, 102**
Mediators	See chemical mediators.	
Melanin	A dark pigment found in melanocytes. Responsible for the pigmentation of the skin.	**81**
Mesenchyme	Embryonic tissue from which connective tissue, smooth muscle and blood vessels arise.	

Metabolic rate	The overall rate at which the reactions for life proceed.	106
Metronidazole	Antimicrobial agent used against anaerobic bacteria and protozoa.	167
Mucopoly-saccharides	A group of carbohydrate compounds that contain hexosamine. When dispersed in water, they make up many of the mucins.	84
Myofibroblast	A differentiated fibroblast with contractile properties.	98
Necrosis/ necrotic	Tissue death. Of individual cells, groups of cells or localised areas of tissue.	87, 96, 103, 105, 113, 120, 126, 130, 140, 161, 168, 170
Neuropathy	Functional disturbance and/or pathological changes affecting the peripheral nervous system.	86
Neutrophil	A white blood cell that ingests bacteria. Type of polymorphonuclear leucocyte or granulocyte.	95, 96
Non-accidental injury	Often to a child or mentally handicapped individual, caused deliberately by another. Attempts are then made to conceal the true nature of the injury.	112
Non-ionic solution	A surface active substance that carries no postive or negative charges and does not absorb into the wound.	160
Occlusive dressing	A type of wound dressing that totally covers the wound bed, sealing it off from the environment. It is impermeable or semi-permeable to moisture.	95, 100, 165, 166
Oedema/ oedematous	Excess tissue fluid.	94, 95, 113, 140, 146, 171, 173
Oncogenesis	The process leading to the formation of tumours.	75
Orthotist	Specialist in the production and use of appliance or apparatus to improve function.	147
Osteomyelitis	Infection of bone.	128, 137
Phagocytosis	The process by which some cells (phagocytes) engulf bacteria, necrotic material or foreign particles.	97

181

Platelet	Component of blood. Aggregation and activation of platelets lead to the inflammatory phase of wound healing.	92, 95, 99
Polymorphonuclear neutrophil	Type of white blood cell.	96
Polysaccharide beads	Synthetic material used as wound filler.	138
Pressure sore	A wound resulting from excessive or prolonged pressure.	97, 106, 118, 125, 126, 127, 138, 164
Proliferation	Process of tissue repair, by formation of replacement cells and/or matrix.	93, 98, 100, 101, 102, 103, 120, 162
Proprioception	The sense of position. Allows an individual to know how limbs are positioned.	86
Prostacyclin	An arachidonic acid derivitive produced by endothelium and smooth muscle in vessel walls. Inhibits platelet aggregation and is a vasodilator. Acts to maintain vessel patency and localise clot formation.	92
Pulmonary embolism	Event that occurs when a particle of material, such as dislodged blood clot, is trapped by the blood vessels supplying the lung. May lead to infarction (death) of a portion of lung or cardiac arrest due to right heart outflow obstruction.	
Pus	Fluid formed by a mixture of exudate, dead and exhausted macrophages, bacteria.	105, 120
Pyrexia	A rise in body's core temperature.	105
Regeneration	Regrowth of tissue.	83, 100, 119, 139
Rheumatoid arthritis	A type of chronic joint disease involving inflammation of synovial membranes.	77, 124
Rodent ulcer	A locally invasive tumour arising in the skin, which frequently presents as an area that fails to heal. Also called basal cell carcinoma. Rarely metastatic.	121
Scab	Coagulum of serum and debris.	96, 165
Scurvy	Deficiency disease resulting from lack of vitamin C.	99

182

Sebum	Secretion produced by sebaceous glands.	81, 85
Septicaemia	Systemic disease. Pathogenic micro-organisms or other toxins are present and persist in the bloodstream.	105, 119, 172, 173
Sequestrum	Separated portion of dead bone.	
Serine proteases	Important family of protein enzymes with roles in digestion, clotting and other processes.	
Silicone foam	Dressing material supplied as two liquids, which on mixing form a foam. This foam sets in the shape of the wound.	138
Skin graft	Portion of skin removed from its natural position. When re-sited elsewhere it must develop a new blood supply.	83, 98, 119, 123, 139, 162
Squame	Flattened, keratin-rich cellular remnant of epidermal cells. Scales found on the outermost layers of the skin.	83
Steroids	Family of compounds used for their anti-inflammatory action. Wide range of systemic effects.	94, 102, 130
Subcuticular	Situated beneath the epidermis. Often applied to a buried suture, placed in the cut dermal edges of a wound.	113
Synergic	Acting together or in harmony.	120
Telangiectasia	A group of dilated capillaries and small arteries.	130
Thrombin	Insoluble protein derived from soluble precursor prothrombin, present in serum.	92
Toxin	Compound which has a toxic or detrimental effect on living cells.	104, 161
Transferrin	Serum protein involved in the transport of iron in the blood.	106
Transpiration	Rate at which a dressing transmits fluid from the wound to the atmosphere.	166
Triceps	Muscle of the posterier aspect of the upper arm.	106

The Wound Programme

An international group of experts provides answers to six fundamental questions about wound management

International Committee on Wound Management

Consensus Statement

1 What is wound management?

1.1 Wound management is the pursuit of the permanent, functional and aesthetic healing of the patient's wound through the promotion of physiological healing and the prevention or elimination of factors - whether local, systemic or external - that disturb healing.

1.2 The means of healing must be conducted by scientifically based procedures and materials. These should be carried out and applied by a properly trained multi-disciplinary team.

1.3 Good wound management focuses not only on the closing of the wound by procedures and dressings but also upon the mental and physical comfort of the patient throughout the process of healing. In addition, the prevention of disfiguring scars, the generation of functional new tissue and prevention of regression are an integral part of wound management.

1.4 It is recognised that there is a group of patients with tissue defects that cannot be healed. The management of these patients should be directed towards the control of pain, treatment of correctable complications and improved quality of life.

2 For the various sub-groups of patients, what are the standard treatment procedures we have to compare with? Are they effective, do they prevent infection or do they interfere with the quality of life?

2.1 In acute wounds, the repercussions on the patient and the patient's life should be assessed. These should consider the patient's condition. The methods of acute treatment should be adaptable according to the established surgical principles of treatment for each different type of acute wound.

2.2 For chronic wounds, the aetiological approach must prevail before treatment is started. There is an urgent need for internationally accepted standards with which new treatment modalities can be compared for their effectiveness, prevention of infection and effect on quality of life

2.3 The effectiveness of the treatment should be assessed objectively.

3 Has effective wound management changed and progressed over the last decade? Is it perceived to have changed?

3.1 Better results have been obtained in wound management in the last decade. These have been achieved by better insights in epidemiology, improved awareness and understanding of the physiological and pathophysiological underlying mechanisms. The result has been improved materials, devices, dressings and techniques.

3.2 More healthcare providers are using modern materials and procedures, but there is still room for improvement.

3.3 While the perception of the change in effective wound management is obvious among healthcare professionals involved in the field, there is a need to increase general awareness of these changes.

4 What are the benefits and cost of the various different forms of wound management?

4.1 The welfare of the patient supercedes the issue of cost. Cost should not be an absolute issue when a life or a limb is at stake.

4.2 The multi-disciplinary approach to patients with wounds can provide many benefits for the patient, the patient's family and society. This is seen in terms of better and timely closure of the wound, in prevention of infection, pain control and good functional and aethetic results.

4.3 There are difficulties in defining what constitutes a benefit in wound management and this may differ from one speciality to another. The patient may also have a different concept of 'benefit'.

4.4 The cost-benefit ratios of the various treatments of different wounds have not been studied sufficiently to enable a consensus on their relative merits. There is an urgent need for a methodology to be developed to enable this to be studied properly.

5 What are the responsibilities of healthcare professionals for patients and their carers?

5.1 The healthcare professions must ensure that their members are well trained at all levels by continuing their education, by being aware of follow-up results of good quality clinical research and by developing appropriate educational material.

5.2 The support of independent educational projects by grants from the wound care industry and other external sources should be welcome.

5.3 Further research should be undertaken with support from professional organisations, universities, and governments. Ethical clinical trials of promising new products should be encouraged.

5.4 The patient, the patient's family and the public should also be informed about the prevention of wounds and the importance of appropriate treatment.

5.5 Primary healthcare providers are in a good position to screen opportunistically for patients at particular risk of wounds and give appropriate advice.

5.6 Government agencies, charitable bodies, patient organisations and the media also have a role to play in the dissemination of information.

6 What are the responsibilities of the authorities in recommendations for wound care, costs, new therapeutics (drugs, devices, etc.)?

6.1 In the face of the growing budgetary implications of health care, authorities responsible for the functioning of the healthcare system should be adequately informed as to the epidemiology of chronic and acute wounds and their social and economic repercussions.

6.2 Authorities responsible for healthcare should ensure that a service for wound care is available and functions effectively.

6.3 Financial resources should be spent as effectively as possible not only on active patient care, but also on the personnel, their training, the continuation of their training, their equipment and facilities. Resources should also be allocated for prevention programmes.

6.4 The curriculum in basic training of healthcare professionals should adequately cover wound care.

6.5 The authorities should facilitate the development of a concise and uniform international classification of wounds and wound management.

6.6 There should be clear legislation on the scientific proof of therapeutic claims and for the quality and safety control of all new materials used in wound care. Adequate legal protection of patent rights of new developments should be ensured.

Good luck with your studies

188